BUILDING
SUSTAINABLE
LEADERSHIP
CAPACITY

The Soul of Educational Leadership

Alan M. Blankstein, Paul D. Houston, Robert W. Cole, Editors

Volume 1: Engaging EVERY Learner

Volume 2: Out-of-the-Box Leadership

Volume 3: Sustaining Professional Learning Communities

Volume 4: Spirituality in Educational Leadership

Volume 5: Building Sustainable Leadership Capacity

Volume 6: Leaders as Communicators and Diplomats

Volume 7: Data-Enhanced Leadership

Volume 8: Leadership for Family and Community Involvement

Volume 9: Leadership for Social Justice and Democracy in Our Schools

Volume 10: Redefining the Role of the Leader: Best Practices Worldwide

Volume 11: Leadership for 21st Century Schools

Volume 12: Transparent Leadership

Volume 13: Looking to the Future (Schools of Our Dreams)

THE SOUL OF EDUCATIONAL LEADERSHIP

VOLUME 5

BUILDING SUSTAINABLE LEADERSHIP CAPACITY

ALAN M. BLANKSTEIN ❧ PAUL D. HOUSTON ❧ ROBERT W. COLE

EDITORS

A JOINT PUBLICATION

American Association of
School Administrators

CORWIN PRESS
A SAGE Company
Thousand Oaks, CA 91320

For information:

Corwin
A SAGE Company
2455 Teller Road
Thousand Oaks, California 91320
(800) 233-9936
Fax: (800) 417-2466
www.corwinpress.com

SAGE Ltd.
1 Oliver's Yard
55 City Road
London EC1Y 1SP
United Kingdom

SAGE India Pvt. Ltd.
B 1/I 1 Mohan Cooperative
    Industrial Area
Mathura Road,
New Delhi 110 044
India

SAGE Asia-Pacific Pte. Ltd.
33 Pekin Street #02-01
Far East Square
Singapore 048763

Printed in the United States of America.

Library of Congress Cataloging-in-Publication Data

Building sustainable leadership capacity/[edited by] Alan M.Blankstein, Paul D. Houston, Robert W. Cole.
    p. cm. — (The soul of educational leadership; v. 5)
"A joint publication with the HOPE Foundation and the American Association of School Administrators."
Includes bibliographical references and index.
ISBN 978-1-4129-4935-4 (cloth)
ISBN 978-1-4129-4936-1 (pbk.)
    1. School administrators—Training of—United States. 2. Educational leadership—United States. I. Blankstein, Alan M., 1959- II. Houston, Paul D. III. Cole, Robert W., 1945- IV. Hope Foundation. V. American Association of School Administrators. VI. Title. VII. Series.

LB2831.82.B85 2009
371.200973—dc22   2009004910

This book is printed on acid-free paper.

09   10   11   12   13   10   9   8   7   6   5   4   3   2   1

Acquisitions Editor:	Debra Stollenwerk
Associate Editor:	Julie McNall
Production Editor:	Libby Larson
Copy Editor:	Teresa Herlinger
Typesetter:	C&M Digitals (P) Ltd.
Proofreader:	Theresa Kay
Indexer:	Maria Sosnowski
Cover Designer:	Michael Dubowe

CONTENTS

ACKNOWLEDGMENTS

Corwin gratefully acknowledges the contributions of the following reviewers:

David M. Dunaway
Assistant Professor of Educational Leadership
University of North Carolina at Charlotte
Charlotte, NC

Sheila Eller
Middle School Principal
Mounds View School District
North Oaks, MN

Theodore J. Kowalski
Kuntz Family Endowed Chair in Educational Administration
University of Dayton
Dayton, OH

ABOUT THE EDITORS

Paul D. Houston served as executive director of the American Association of School Administrators (AASA) from 1994 to 2008. He currently serves as president of the Center for Empowered Leadership (CFEL).

Dr. Houston has established himself as one of the leading spokespersons for American education through his extensive speaking engagements, published articles, and his regular appearances on national radio and television.

Dr. Houston has coauthored three books: *Exploding the Myths*, with Joe Schneider; *The Board-Savvy Superintendent*, with Doug Eadie; and *The Spiritual Dimension of Leadership*, with Steven Sokolow. He has also authored three books: *Articles of Faith and Hope for Public Education*, *Outlooks and Perspectives on American Education*, and *No Challenge Left Behind: Transforming America's Schools Through Heart and Soul*.

Dr. Houston worked previously as a teacher and building administrator in North Carolina and New Jersey. He has also served as assistant superintendent in Birmingham, Alabama, and as superintendent of schools in Princeton, New Jersey; Tucson, Arizona; and Riverside, California.

Dr. Houston has also served in an adjunct capacity for the University of North Carolina, Harvard University, Brigham Young University, and Princeton University. He has been a consultant and speaker throughout the United States and overseas, and he has published more than 200 articles in professional journals.

Alan M. Blankstein is founder and president of the HOPE Foundation, a not-for-profit organization whose honorary chair is Nobel Prize winner Archbishop Desmond Tutu. The HOPE Foundation (Harnessing Optimism and Potential through Education) is dedicated to supporting educational leaders over time in creating school cultures where failure is not an option for any student. HOPE sustains student success.

The HOPE Foundation brought W. Edwards Deming and his work to light in educational circles, beginning with the Shaping Chicago's Future conference in 1988. From 1988 to 1992, in a series of Shaping America's Future forums and PBS video conferences, he brought together scores of national and world leaders including Al Shanker; Peter Senge; Mary Futrell; Linda Darling-Hammond; Ed Zigler; and CEOs of GM, Ford, and other corporations to determine how best to bring quality concepts and those of "learning organizations" to bear in educational systems.

The HOPE Foundation provides professional development for thousands of educational leaders annually throughout North America and other parts of the world, including South Africa. HOPE also provides long-term support for school improvement through leadership academies and intensive on-site school change efforts, leading to dramatic increases in student achievement in diverse settings.

A former "high risk" youth, Blankstein began his career in education as a music teacher and has worked within youth-serving organizations for 20 years, including the March of Dimes, Phi Delta Kappa, and the National Educational Service (NES), which he founded in 1987 and directed for 12 years.

He coauthored with Rick DuFour the *Reaching Today's Youth* curriculum, now provided as a course in 16 states, and has contributed writing to *Educational Leadership, School Administrator, Executive Educator, High School Magazine, Reaching Today's Youth,* and *EQ + IQ = Best Leadership Practices for Caring and Successful Schools.* Blankstein has provided keynote presentations and workshops for virtually every major educational organization. He is author of the bestselling book *Failure Is Not an Option™: Six Principles That Guide Student Achievement in High-Performing Schools,* which has been awarded "Book of the Year" by the National Staff Development Council and nominated for three other national and international awards.

Alan Blankstein is on the Harvard International Principals Center's advisory board, has served as a board member for the Federation of Families for Children's Mental Health, is a cochair of Indiana University's Neal Marshall Black Culture Center's Community Network, and is advisor to the Faculty and Staff for Student Excellence mentoring program. He is also an advisory board member for the Forum on Race, Equity, and Human Understanding with the Monroe County Schools in Indiana, and has served on the Board of Trustees for the Jewish Child Care Agency (JCCA), at which he was once a youth-in-residence.

Robert W. Cole is proprietor and founder of Edu-Data, a firm specializing in writing, research, and publication services. He was a member of the staff of *Phi Delta Kappan* magazine for 14 years: assistant editor from 1974–1976, managing editor from 1976–1980, and editor-in-chief from 1981–1988. During his tenure as editor-in-chief, the *Kappan* earned more than 40 Distinguished Achievement Awards from the Association of Educational Publishers, three of them for his editorials.

Since leaving the *Kappan,* Cole has served as founding vice president of the Schlechty Center for Leadership in School Reform (1990–1994). There, he managed district- and communitywide school reform efforts and led the team that created the Kentucky Superintendents' Leadership Institute. He formed the Bluegrass Leadership Network, in which superintendents worked together to use current leadership concepts to solve reform-oriented management and leadership problems.

As senior consultant to the National Reading Styles Institute (1994–2005), Cole served as editor and lead writer of the Power Reading Program. He and a team of writers and illustrators created a series of hundreds of graded short stories, short novels, and comic books from Primer through Grade 10. Those stories were then recorded by Cole and Dr. Marie Carbo; they are being used by schools all across the United States to teach struggling readers.

Cole has served as a book development editor for the Association for Supervision and Curriculum Development (ASCD), for Corwin, and for Writer's Edge Press. He has been president of the Educational Press Association of America and member of the EdPress Board of Directors. He has presented workshops, master classes, and lectures at universities nationwide, including Harvard University, Stanford University, Indiana University, Xavier University, Boise State University, and the University of Southern Maine. He has served as a special consultant to college and university deans in working with faculties on writing for professional publication. Recently, he began serving as managing editor and senior associate with the Center for Empowered Leadership.

ABOUT THE CONTRIBUTORS

Maurice J. Elias is a professor of psychology at Rutgers University; president of the International Society for Community Research and Action/Division of Community Psychology (27) of the American Psychological Association; director of the Rutgers Social-Emotional Learning Lab and the Developing Safe and Civil Schools (DSACS) prevention initiative (www.teachSECD.com); and founding member of the Leadership Team for the Collaborative for Academic, Social, and Emotional Learning (www.CASEL.org). His books include *Emotionally Intelligent Parenting* (2000), *The Social Decision Making/Social Problem Solving Curricula for Elementary and Middle School Students* (2006), *The Educator's Guide to Emotional Intelligence and Academic Achievement: Social-Emotional Learning in the Classroom* (Corwin, 2006), and *Urban Dreams: Stories of Hope, Character, and Resilience* (2008). He also writes a blog on SEL for the George Lucas Foundation at www.edutopia.org. Dr. Elias is a licensed psychologist, an approved provider of professional development for educators in New Jersey (#697), and can be reached at RutgersMJE@aol.com.

Dean Fink is an international educational development consultant. He is a former superintendent and principal with the Halton Board of Education in Ontario, Canada. In his career, he has taught at all levels of education from primary grades to graduate school. He has been a senior manager at both the primary and secondary levels. In the past 14 years, Fink has made presentations or conducted workshops in 31 different countries including the United Kingdom, the United States, Australia, New Zealand, Israel, Russia, Romania,

Ukraine, Ireland, Sweden, Denmark, Turkey, Mongolia, Spain, Singapore, and the Baltic States. He has presented keynote addresses to a number of national and international conferences.

Dean Fink has published numerous book chapters and articles on topics related to school effectiveness, leadership, and change in schools in such journals as *Phi Delta Kappan, Educational Administration Quarterly, Educational Leadership,* the *International Journal of Educational Change,* and *School Effectiveness and School Improvement.* He is the author or coauthor of *Changing Our Schools* (1996) with Louise Stoll of the Institute of Education, *Good Schools/Real Schools: Why School Reform Doesn't Last* (2000), and *It's About Learning and It's About Time* (2003) with Louise Stoll and Lorna Earl of OISE/University of Toronto. His most recent books are *Sustainable Leadership* with Andy Hargreaves (2006) and *Leadership for Mortals: Developing and Sustaining Leaders of Learning* for Corwin/ Paul Chapman (2006). His next book, due in 2009, is *The Succession Challenge: Building Educational Leadership Capacity Through Succession Management* (Sage, Corwin).

Fink has been married and is the father of two daughters who are both teachers, and grandfather to two grandsons, ages 15 and 13. He spends his spare time golfing or waiting for the Canadian golf season to begin.

Michael Fullan is Professor Emeritus of the Ontario Institute for Studies in Education of the University of Toronto. Recognized as a worldwide authority on educational reform, Fullan is engaged in training, consulting, and evaluating change projects around the world, and his books have been published in many languages.

Michael Fullan is currently Special Advisor to the Premier and Minister of Education in Ontario. His book *Leading in a Culture of Change* was given the 2002 Book of the Year Award by the National Staff Development Council, and *Breakthrough* (with Peter Hill and Carmel Crévola) won the 2006 Book of the Year Award from the American Association of Colleges for Teacher Education.

Alma Harris is Chair of Educational Leadership at the Institute of Education, University of London. She has previously held posts at the University of Nottingham and University of Bath. She is currently the associate director of the Specialist Schools and Academies Trust, and she is the editor of *School Leadership and Management.*

Her research work has centered upon organizational change and leadership. She is internationally known for her work on school improvement, focusing particularly on ways in which leadership can contribute to school development and change. Her most recent work is on the role of parental engagement and raising achievement in schools.

For the last 10 years, **David Jackson** has led large-scale programs supporting the implementation of what has come to be called "system leadership"—the leadership of locality approaches and network-based practices.

He is currently a senior associate of the Innovation Unit where, from 2006, he was the lead consultant to the Innovation Unit's Next Practice in System Leadership program, coordinating a team of consultants who work directly with 16 advanced field-trial sites across the country. This work also developed tools and artifacts designed to support radical innovation in the field of locality provision and collaboration. From April 2008, the program was extended to include work in Applied Next Practice. In partnership with the National College for School Leadership (NCSL), the Innovation Unit has also introduced new approaches to support provision of strategic leadership for complex locality change.

Jackson began teaching in 1971 and was for 14 years headteacher of Sharnbrook Upper School and Community College in Bedfordshire, UK, which became nationally recognized for its success in educational innovation. In 2000, he was appointed NCSL's first Director of Research and School Improvement, from 2002 becoming the director of NCSL's Networked Learning Group and Strategic Director of the College. The Group's best known program involved 134 Networked Learning Communities (1,550 schools) across England over a 5-year period. It also promoted innovation in leadership development design, collaborative leadership approaches, network leadership, and models of brokerage and capacity building across local authorities.

David Jackson has taught in master's programs at the Universities of Nottingham and Cambridge, where he was a visiting scholar, including in Cambridge's international MPhil program in Educational Reform and Teacher Development. He has published widely on a range of themes—leadership, school improvement, innovation, enquiry, student voice, Networked Learning Communities, and knowledge management—and has supported school and system improvement programs both in the UK and abroad.

Robert W. Katulak has been a professional educator for over 32 years. He is the Superintendent of Schools in the New Hyde Park-Garden City Park School District in Nassau County, Long Island, in

New York State. He was previously the Assistant Superintendent for Elementary and Middle Level Education in the North Rockland CSD in Rockland County, New York. He was an elementary principal and teacher for over 19 years prior to that. He is currently a national trainer for the Marie Carbo National Reading Styles Institute.

In addition to his professional experience, he is an actor and a singer in regional theater and for charitable benefits. He is a theater buff and gardener and believes in the power of family ties. He has been married to his lovely wife, Johanna, for over 30 years and is the proud father of a college graduate—his son, Robert Christopher. He is currently putting the finishing touches on a musical based on the life of President Andrew Jackson called *Old Hickory.*

Linda Lambert is Professor Emeritus at California State University, East Bay, and founder of Lambert Leadership Development. Lambert has served in multiple leadership roles including principal and director of numerous reform initiatives and academies. Her pioneering work in leadership has led to invitations by the U.S. State Department, foreign ministries, and the Rockefeller Foundation to consult in Egypt, Asia, Australia, Canada, and Mexico. In addition to numerous articles and book chapters, Lambert is the lead author of the 1995 and 2002 best-selling texts, *The Constructivist Leader* (lst and 2nd editions) and *Who Will Save Our Schools?* (1997); author of *Building Leadership Capacity in Schools* (1998); *Developing Leadership Capacity for School Improvement,* an adaptation of the 1998 text published in London (2003); and *Leadership Capacity for Lasting School Improvement* (2003). Her awards include International Book of the Year for *The Constructivist Leader,* given by the National Staff Development Council (NSDC) and ASCD; Outstanding California Educator; and Professor of the Year. Her major consulting and research areas involve constructivist leadership, leadership capacity, women in leadership, and organizational development. Lambert is now a novelist living in Northern California.

More than 30 years ago, **Nancy Shin Pascal** began her lifelong career of service teaching junior high French. She subsequently served as a social worker and an analyst for GTE before returning to education in 1988, as Executive Director of the HOPE Foundation.

As Executive Director of HOPE, Nancy Shin Pascal leads the long-term professional development services of the foundation in 15 states,

Canada, and the Hopi Nation. Her work has consistently led to increases in student proficiency on standardized tests across geographies, race, and economic status. Over the last 2 years, Nancy has used the Failure Is Not an Option Professional Learning Communities of HOPE approach in urban Milwaukee, Wisconsin, and in the poorest county in California. In both cases, student proficiency levels have increased substantially. For example, sixth-grade students in Milwaukee scoring "proficient or above" in math rose from 1 percent to 34 percent. Likewise in California, fourth-grade students scoring "proficient or above" in language arts increased from 5 percent to 23 percent.

Nancy Shin Pascal has helped create award-winning publications and video programs including *Reclaiming Youth at Risk*, *Discipline With Dignity*, and *Reconnecting Youth*. She has coproduced PBS and C-SPAN productions on *Breaking the Cycle of Violence*, as well as *Creating Learning Organizations* with Peter Senge and Dr. W. Edwards Deming. She recently contributed to *Sustaining Professional Learning Communities*, Volume 3 of *The Soul of Educational Leadership* series (Corwin). She also has directed professional development for upwards of 30,000 educators annually. In addition, Nancy serves as a reviewer for the North Central Regional Educational Laboratory.

Nancy Shin Pascal's dedication to helping leaders assure success for all children has included serving as a FASE (Faculty And Students for Excellence) mentor at Indiana University and fundraising for international mission work. Nancy has two successful children, who now reside on opposite coasts of the United States.

Dennis Sparks serves as a "thinking partner" to leadership teams of education organizations that are committed to the continuous improvement of teaching and learning for all students. He is Emeritus Executive Director of the National Staff Development Council, having served as its executive director from 1984–2007. Sparks has spoken to countless educational groups and published on a wide variety of subjects in most major educational publications. His most recent book is *Leading for Results: Transforming Teaching, Learning, and Relationships in Schools*. His professional purpose is the dramatic improvement in the quality of leadership, teaching, and learning in schools so that all students thrive academically and are surrounded by supportive relationships.

Louise Stoll is a past president of the International Congress for School Effectiveness and School Improvement (ICSEI). She is currently Visiting Professor at the London, Centre for Leadership in Learning at the Institute of Education, University of London, and at the Department of Education, University of Bath, where she was Professor in Education and Director of its Centre for Leadership, Learning and Change. Previously, she was a primary school teacher and researcher in inner London, research director in an Ontario school district, and Co-ordinating Director of the International School Effectiveness and Improvement Centre at the Institute of Education, where she established the School Improvement Network. Her research and development activity in England and internationally has increasingly focused on how individuals, groups, organizations, and systems collaborate to create capacity for learning and improvement and the leadership required for this to happen. Author and editor of many publications including *Professional Learning Communities* (coedited with Karen Seashore Louis) and *It's About Learning and It's About Time* with Dean Fink and Lorna Earl, Stoll also presents and consults in many countries.

INTRODUCTION

ROBERT W. COLE

I n 2006 we began this multivolume series, *The Soul of Educational Leadership,* with two vitally important themes: inclusiveness (in *Engaging Every Learner*) and transformation (in *Out-of-the-Box Leadership*). In Volume 3, *Sustaining Professional Learning Communities,* we moved on to the perilously difficult task of holding onto, and improving upon, valuable work once it has begun. Now, 2 years later, after tackling *Spirituality in Educational Leadership* (Volume 4) and *The Leader as Communicator and Diplomat* (Volume 6), we address *Building Sustainable Leadership Capacity,* a topic that feels like the first cousin of Volume 3.

In education, it's always been a challenge to retain the good things we've accomplished. So often, years of good work can be blown into oblivion by a new superintendent, or a turnover on the school board, or budget woes, or the latest craze in professional development. Always at the heart of this perennial struggle are the young people who matter so deeply to those of us who work in and around schools, and to our society. That theme was sounded in Volume 1 by Alan Blankstein—editor of this series, together with myself and Paul Houston: "Saving young people from failure in school is equivalent to saving their lives!" That truth set the tone for this entire series. We know how to do what needs doing, and the aim of these volumes is to enlist the thinking of those who set the tone for the discussion—in this case, holding onto the excellence that we have caused to happen.

This volume provides a range of complementary viewpoints from around the world. The authors herein see clearly that the development of leadership capacity that will endure requires a clarity of shared moral vision and urgency, leadership in community, and a recognition of the challenges posed by young people's lives outside of school. Moreover, as Dennis Sparks puts it, "Leadership development supports leaders in developing a sense of appreciation and hopefulness and in leading from their strengths and 'best selves.'" That moral framework is consonant with the vision that has guided this series from its inception.

Sparks, emeritus executive director of the National Staff Development Council whose most recent book is *Leading for Results: Transforming Teaching, Learning, and Relationships in Schools,* leads off this volume with a call to arms in "What I Believe About Leadership Development." "Without teamwork and sustained professional learning," he writes, "systemwide continuous improvements are fated to remain a fervent wish rather than become a reality." Sparks provides an ideal frame for this volume when he emphasizes that "significant improvements in teaching and learning for all students begins with significant change in leaders."

Leadership as it is traditionally conceived has little appeal to the world's emerging leaders, maintains Linda Lambert in "Reconceptualizing the Road Toward Leadership Capacity." Professor Emeritus at California State University, East Bay, and founder of Lambert Leadership Development (and now a novelist), Lambert asks what kind of leadership survives when the formal leader leaves. Her answer is this: leadership reconceived as reciprocal, purposeful learning in community and realized as the network of learning relationships in an organization.

In "The Moral Imperative Revisited: Achieving Large-Scale Reform," Michael Fullan urges educators to integrate an urgent moral purpose with appropriate strategies to achieve that purpose, and thus benefit entire systems, as well as individual students and schools. Fullan, Professor Emeritus of the Ontario Institute for Studies in Education at the University of Toronto and an internationally recognized authority on education reform, emphasizes that a moral imperative must be combined with powerful strategies to make it a reality *in practice*. When this happens, moral purpose takes on a life of its own, thus giving it additional power in the hearts and minds of all educators and even the public.

The organizational structures of most schools around the world are fundamentally unchanged since the beginning of the 20th century, maintains Dean Fink in "Leadership for Mortals: Developing and Sustaining Leaders of Learning." Fink, an international educational development consultant and a former superintendent and principal with the Halton Board of Education in Ontario, Canada, notes that policy efforts focusing on results have placed unique pressures on leaders, and undermined educational leadership. The challenge for today's leaders is to cope with outmoded structures while simultaneously leading schools on the path toward becoming learning communities.

Louise Stoll and David Jackson emphasize that leadership has to be a shared enterprise, within and between its various levels. "It has to be a system that connects, not divides," they write in "Liberating Leadership Potential: Designing for Leadership Growth." To make this happen requires the development of leadership capacity. Stoll is Visiting Professor at the London Centre for Leadership in Learning at the Institute of Education, University of London, and also at the Department of Education, University of Bath. Jackson, senior associate of the Innovation Unit, has in recent years led large-scale programs supporting the implementation of what has come to be called "system leadership."

"The bond between social class and educational achievement is a particularly powerful one, and particularly resistant to change," writes Alma Harris in "Against the Odds: Successful Leadership in Challenging Schools." Harris, Chair of Educational Leadership at the Institute of Education, University of London, continues, "Breaking this bond will require leadership that is responsive to school context and is underpinned by an unrelenting focus on improving conditions at the building and classroom levels." Leaders in such settings will need "a strong sense of moral purpose and a firm belief that schools and young people can achieve against all odds."

"Leadership must be shared; it can no longer reside solely in the hands of a superintendent or a building principal," writes Robert W. Katulak, superintendent of schools in the New Hyde Park-Garden City Park School District in Nassau County, Long Island. In "Developing Leaders of Learners," Katulak details the ways in which he ensured that leadership was entrusted to teachers—"leaders of learners who are created from within." The mark of success for any leader is if their work is sustained after they leave an organization, he concludes; a true leader knows that if he or she modeled shared leadership correctly, other leaders will know how to imitate this model.

In "Building Leadership Capacity for School-Based Social-Emotional Learning (SEL): The Trajectory of Young Leaders," Maurice J. Elias, professor in the psychology department at Rutgers University and founding member of the leadership team for the Collaborative for Academic, Social, and Emotional Learning (CASEL), allowed four up-and-coming educational leaders to tell their own stories. The result is an intersection of two goals: "understanding important influences in the emergence of leadership at a relatively early point in the leadership trajectory, and providing an opportunity for young leaders to share their particular stories."

Nancy Shin Pascal, executive director of the HOPE Foundation, writes the capstone piece for this volume: "Developing and Sustaining Leadership Capacity." Taking into account the great demand for leaders caused by retirements and mobility, she provides a detailed examination of the structures and processes used by the district leadership to recruit future leaders and build leadership capacity at all levels in Mattoon, a small district in east-central Illinois. The intent of Mattoon's leaders was this: to build the leadership capacity necessary to ensure the success of *all* their students and to address the looming retirement of a daunting percentage of the entire staff. As Shin Pascal concludes, "Developing teacher leadership is a very practical response to the harsh realities of instability of leadership at the top, escalating student needs, and decreasing resources."

Back in Volume 3, whose themes echoed this volume, Nancy Shin Pascal and Alan Blankstein, reporting on their work in Newport News, Virginia, wrote of the need for "constancy of purpose" in bringing about change that endures. They concluded, "The journey is not over, and never will be." So it is for leaders in education, whose work of preparing young people for life includes both unique rewards and trying sacrifices. The work never ends, but the rewards both for self and for society are immeasurably grand. As always, it is our aim to help strengthen you for this task.

CHAPTER ONE

WHAT I BELIEVE ABOUT LEADERSHIP DEVELOPMENT

DENNIS SPARKS

S ustained and well-designed leadership development is essential in school systems that desire high-quality teaching and learning for all students in all classrooms. Such leadership development prepares leaders to be *instructional* and to create school cultures that promote continuous improvements in teaching and learning and surround both young people and adults with supportive relationships.

The pressures created by high standards and testing requirements and the guidance provided by long-range planning are insufficient in themselves to continuously improve teaching and learning across a school system. Instead, such improvements will occur through the development of teamwork, "real time" professional learning, and the creation of system and school cultures in which new ideas and practices can grow and flourish. Without teamwork and sustained

> *Without teamwork and sustained professional learning, systemwide continuous improvements are fated to remain a fervent wish rather than become a reality.*

professional learning, systemwide continuous improvements are fated to remain a fervent wish rather than become a reality.

It is critically important that teamwork and high-quality professional learning begin at the highest leadership levels in a school system and that district leaders be fully committed to and engaged in their own development. Significant change throughout the system requires that leaders be willing and able to change their own beliefs, understanding, and actions.

The kind of team-based "real time" professional learning I advocate for leaders is very different from the "sit-and-get" sessions still commonly experienced by the vast majority of school and district administrators. Such activities—which sometimes are little more than a series of speakers who offer their viewpoints on a variety of subjects—are often markedly separate from leaders' core day-to-day responsibilities, seldom build on one another to develop complex understandings and skills, do little to promote teamwork within the school system, and reinforce the mistaken notion that good staff development is a series of "presenters" who "convey" ideas and research to relatively passive recipients.

I Believe

Based on more than 40 years of experience as an educator (with more than 30 of those years dedicated to the field of professional learning), my careful reading of the professional literature in education and related fields, and conversations with thousands of administrators and teachers from a variety of settings, I have acquired a number of beliefs about leadership and leadership development. I offer these beliefs in the spirit of dialogue as propositions for leadership development. I encourage leaders to examine their own "truths" in these areas and to consider their implications for their day-to-day learning and actions.

- *I believe that significant improvements in teaching and learning for all students begin with significant change in leaders.* Therefore, leadership development focuses on affecting what leaders believe, understand, say, and do each day. Leadership development is sufficiently robust that it literally changes the brains of leaders as they acquire new beliefs, deepen their understanding of important subjects, and develop new habits.

- *I believe that the quality of relationships in schools profoundly affects the quality of teaching and learning.* Therefore, leadership development creates relationships among leaders that inspire hope rather than resignation, provides support in implementing new practices, and inspires the courage necessary to consistently act in ways that promote the welfare of all young people.

- *I believe that individuals working interdependently in teams pursuing goals that stretch their capacities can accomplish far more than individuals working alone.* Therefore, leadership development engages leaders in genuine teamwork based on ambitious goals for student learning as a primary means of continuous improvement that overcomes the centrifugal forces of professional isolation.

- *I believe that if all students are to experience high-quality teaching and learning and be surrounded by supportive relationships, so too must their teachers be surrounded by such relationships and experience continuous "real time" professional learning.* Therefore, leadership development equips leaders with the knowledge and skills to create high-performance teams and to embed professional learning in teachers' daily work lives.

- *I believe that continuous improvements in teaching and learning require that leaders create cultures of clarity, cohesion, integrity, candor, teamwork, trust, and interpersonal accountability.* Therefore, leadership development cultivates those qualities in and among leaders so that they, in turn, can lead in the creation of such cultures in schools.

- *I believe that leaders' authenticity and integrity are among their most important leadership "tools."* Therefore, leadership development promotes leaders' understanding of their most important values, purposes, and ideas. Likewise, leadership development supports leaders' ability to act with high levels of integrity so that their words and actions are widely and deeply respected.

- *I believe that leaders' interior lives are a source of inspiration and guidance.* Therefore, leadership development equips leaders with reflective techniques such as journal writing and reading of biographies and provides methods by which leaders can still their minds to increase awareness of deeper sources of wisdom and knowing.

————— ✦ —————

Leadership development supports leaders in developing a sense of appreciation and hopefulness and in leading from their strengths and "best selves."

• *I believe that leaders' feelings are contagious and affect the emotional welfare of the organizations they lead.* Therefore, leadership development supports leaders in developing a sense of appreciation and hopefulness and in leading from their strengths and "best selves."

• *I believe that effective leadership is a matter of heart and spirit as well as the head.* Therefore, leadership development enables leaders to speak from both their hearts and heads about their values, purposes, and ideas, to the hearts and heads of the school community rather than through the exercise of force and fear.

• *I believe that the vast majority of leaders know more about effective leadership than they regularly practice.* Therefore, leadership development provides opportunities for leaders to identify prior knowledge and to set goals to translate that knowledge into new habits of mind and behavior.

• *I believe that leadership is primarily an expression of numerous habits of mind and behavior.* Therefore, leadership development provides opportunities for leaders to practice new ways of thinking and acting until they become habitual.

• *I believe that learning is most powerful when "doing" is integrated into the learning process.* Therefore, most leadership development occurs as leaders engage with their peers in the core tasks of their work—for instance, visiting classrooms to ascertain the quality of student learning, talking with teachers about teaching, or leading learning-oriented meetings.

• *I believe that leaders' assumptions and conceptual frameworks have a large effect on their day-to-day practice, often in ways that are invisible.* Therefore, leadership development assists leaders in surfacing their current assumptions and frameworks and in altering them to support the achievement of organizational goals.

- *I believe that dialogue-based conversations are a powerful and underused means of promoting professional learning and collaboration.* Therefore, leadership development teaches the skills of committed listening—a fundamental quality of learning-oriented conversations—and of surfacing assumptions in the spirit of mutual learning and influence.

- *I believe that the solutions to most problems of teaching and learning require creation and invention rather than prescription or duplication.* Therefore, leadership development promotes attitudes and habits of mind that enable flexible thinking and the conceptualization of alternative futures.

- *I believe that improvement is ultimately about turning ideas into a stream of actions that produce intended results.* Therefore, leadership development cultivates the habit of consistently moving learning and planning into action to continuously close the gaps between what is known and intended and what is done.

Because I believe that the overarching and intertwined moral purposes of schools are to enable all students to develop to their full potential and to create the next generation of informed and engaged world citizens, I want all leaders to possess the understanding and skills necessary to serve as members and leaders of the high-functioning teams that are essential in creating such schools. And because I believe that what leaders understand, say, and do each day matters, I feel strongly that the kind of learning I have described is a matter of the utmost importance and urgency.

CHAPTER TWO

RECONCEPTUALIZING THE ROAD TOWARD LEADERSHIP CAPACITY

LINDA LAMBERT

In the spring of 2007, I taught a workshop on "Women's Ways of Leading" to a group of 45 Moslem women in the Genting Highlands in Malaysia. The women were engaged, forthright, and smart, and I came to feel that they had increased their skills and confidence as leaders.

Near the end of our time together, one of the more outspoken women said, "But I don't want to be a leader." When I asked her why not, she replied, "Because leaders are in charge. They tell others what to do, and they often don't listen." I turned to the other women in the room and asked, "How many of you feel the same way?" Many hands went up. When I realized my mistake, I told them my definition of leadership. The first woman spoke again: "If leadership is to be defined in that way, of course I would want to be a leader. We all would." As I looked around the room, one after the other the women smiled.

How could I have forgotten? I've encountered this situation before in other countries, but also in the United States. Traditional leadership has little appeal to the world's emerging leaders. How could it?

❖ ❖ ❖

Traditional leadership comes in many forms, but at its heart is the belief that there are only certain individuals who can lead.

Traditional leadership comes in many forms, but at its heart is the belief that there are only certain individuals who can lead. They are invariably anointed with formal authority—narrowly defined roles, and special qualities, characteristics, and acquired skills meant to control, influence, manipulate, or involve others. (Formal authority is not in itself a bad thing, so long as it does not exclude others from leading.) In most cases, they are perceived to be "born leaders." For decades, the major writings on leadership from people such as Michael Fullan, Tom Peters, Jim Collins, Rudy Giuliani, and Lee Iacocca have suggested qualities that leaders must possess: charisma, perseverance, creativity, character, curiosity. Certainly these qualities are desirable, but do they not exist in some measure in all of us? It is the evocative learning environment that individuals experience—not some innate predestination—that arouses these and many other desirable leadership traits. The masses of individuals who come into contact with "leaders" may find them to be autocratic and demanding, or kind and benevolent, or thoughtful and engaging. These masses tend to direct their attentions and energies toward figuring out what their leaders want of them. Even the most enlightened leader is viewed as a singular individual, unique in his or her character—unique enough that the club is deemed to be exclusive.

And, when these leaders leave, most often the organization retreats to its former self.[1] Worse still, the individuals within the organization are left wounded and confused.

More than a decade ago, attention began to gravitate to the concept of "leadership capacity." Neither "leadership" nor "capacity" was a new concept. Combine them, however, and the meaning changes. Two primary forms of capacity have since emerged: the personal and the organizational. Personal definitions of capacity relate to the leadership potential of individuals. On the other hand, I have consistently defined leadership capacity as an organizational concept: *broad-based, skillful participation in the work of leadership* (Lambert, 2003). This definition envisions leadership capacity as the dynamic interaction between skill and participation patterns among all members of the organization in the performance of leadership conversations and actions (see Figure 2.1). Expectations for full participation require that invitations be extended to those who have hesitated to see themselves as leaders in the past.

The core of this discussion of leadership capacity rests with the phrase, "in the work of leadership." The crucial modifier, "broad-based, skillful participation," is how leadership is defined. If traditional leadership holds fast, clinging to varying renditions of leadership capacity, it becomes *faux* leadership capacity. And *authentic* leadership capacity becomes an unreachable goal.

THE WORK OF LEADERSHIP: A CONSTRUCTIVIST VIEW

So what is meant by "the work of leadership" within the context of leadership capacity? What was it that persuaded the women in the Malaysian workshop to change their minds about their own identity as leaders? What kind of leadership survives when the formal leader leaves?

In *The Constructivist Leader* (Lambert et al., 2002), the perspective on leadership separates the notion of leadership from the individual alone and invokes broader perspectives and systemic thought. When leadership is understood as *reciprocal, purposeful learning in community,* the notion of leadership is transmuted into the network of learning relationships in an organization. This concept relies on equitable relationships, the exercise of collaboration, moral purpose, and engaged learning communities. The approaches involved in *leading as a form of learning* consist of community visioning, communicating, learning, relating, and sustaining—the very dynamics that make leadership capacity possible.

Reciprocity enables the pursuit of learning and leading within patterns of relationships in which individuals are mutually committed to each other, rather than playing dominant or submissive roles. For instance, when two leaders enter into a peer-coaching relationship,

Principal's Level of Participation

Depth of Leadership Skills and Understandings

	Low	High
High	**Quadrant 1** • Principal as autocratic manager • Limited (one-way) flow of information; no shared vision • Codependent, paternal/maternal relationships; rigidly defined roles • Norms of compliance, blame; program coherence technical and superficial • Lack of innovation in teaching and learning • Student achievement is poor, or showing short-term improvements on standardized measures	**Quadrant 2** • Principal as "laissez-faire" manager; many teachers developing unrelated programs • Fragmentation and lack of coherence of information, and programs' lack of shared purpose • Norms of individualism, lack of collective responsibility • Undefined roles and responsibilities • Spotty innovation with both excellent and poor classrooms • Student achievement appears static overall (unless data are disaggregated)
Low	**Quadrant 3** • Principal and key teachers as purposeful leadership team • Limited uses of schoolwide data, information flow within designated leadership groups • Polarized staff, pockets of strong resistance • Designated leaders act efficiently; others serve in traditional roles • Strong reflection, innovation, and teaching excellence among selected teachers; program coherence still weak • Student achievement static or showing slight improvement	**Quadrant 4** • Principal and teachers, as well as parents and students, are skillful leaders • Shared vision results in program coherence • Inquiry-based use of information to inform decisions and practice • Roles and actions reflect broad involvement, collaboration, and collective responsibility • Reflective practice consistently leads to innovation • Student achievement is high or improving steadily

Depth of Leadership Skills and Understandings

Principal's Level of Participation

Figure 2.1 Leadership Capacity of Four School Types

they commit to the mutuality of learning. When a school leadership team engages its members in deep dialogue toward shared understandings, reciprocal learning enables the team to be smarter than any one of its members. The brain's capacity to find patterns and make sense of the world is liberated within such relationships that encourage mutual care and equitable engagement. Learning is constructivist, in that individuals construct meanings from the new patterns and connections created through conversations, inquiry, and coaching. This emancipatory "social contract" reshapes the patterns of relationships within which learning and leading take place, freeing minds to explore openly with others. Without reciprocity and constructed meanings, the balance of power is tilted. In some situations, such as the military, this imbalance is essential to a situation based on unified, efficient action ensured by obedience. However, if relationships such as marriage, social institutions such as schools, or governing approaches such as democracy lack reciprocal structures, the result is disengagement; apathy; and retreat into focus on the self, prejudice, and fear.

While learning and leading are, by their very nature, *purposeful,* morally engaged purpose is more than survival-driven purpose. To be morally engaged in the world requires that individuals bring to the surface and examine those values, perspectives, and understandings that inform moment-to-moment actions, the treatment of others, and visions for a better world—that is, equity, democracy, human rights, caring, and social justice. When behaviors are value-based, discrepancies can provoke outrage; actors cannot rest without addressing the differences observed. For instance, when school leaders claim to value learning for all and the evidence suggests that this is not occurring—that a yawning gap in achievement exists—a staff can rightly experience moral outrage. Groups and individuals are then driven to find and work toward solutions or experience remorse. A sense of justice and care leads to investment in and tenacity about actions intended to right a wrong or create a better future. This is purposeful learning.

Moreover, learning and leadership occur in *community.* This community can be as intimate as an organization, a neighborhood, or a school. A community can be a gathering of kindred souls or friends. Ultimately, a community is related to that which is most human: the children of the world, those brought into relationship by tragedy, those who are joined by oppression, those joined by a share purpose. Such lived experiences also encompass the dailiness of lives, the moment-to-moment interactions, and the meaningful dialogue and growing self-awareness we hold about who is included and the actions taken to achieve purposeful lives.

Everyone has the right, the ability, and the responsibility to lead—for leading means engaging in learning through the process of change. Leading enables everyone to realize meaning and purpose rather than waiting for others to find it for them. When everyone takes responsibility for leading, the manifestation of values is brought into existence, participants are awake to possibilities, and they are fully *present* in the world. Rita, a teacher at Easton High School in Seattle, explains it this way:

—— ✄ ——

Everyone has the right, the ability, and the responsibility to lead—for leading means engaging in learning through the process of change. Leading enables everyone to realize meaning and purpose rather than waiting for others to find it for them.

> I view myself as simply one small part of the wheel that turns; at times I am the hub, at times one of the spokes, and at times the rim that meets the road. . . . I believe in the intrinsic good of people and look at my job as helping them to see that within themselves.

Such "presence" has long been seen as an individual spiritual journey, yet when this journey occurs within a reciprocal and purposeful learning community, presence can be a collective achievement (Senge, Scharmer, Jaworski, & Flowers, 2004).

The discussion of leadership above brings us to the following assumptions:

1. Leadership is not trait theory; leadership and leader are not the same.

2. Leadership is about the learning that leads to constructive change. Leadership has direction toward a shared purpose.

3. Everyone has the potential, the right, and the responsibility to be a leader. Leading is skilled and complicated work that every member of the school community can learn. Democracy defines the rights of individuals to actively participate in the decisions that affect their lives.

4. Leading is a shared endeavor, the foundation for the democratization of schools. Leading for school change is done most effectively in the presence of others.

5. Leadership requires the redistribution of power and authority; reciprocity is an essential condition of this process.

6. How leadership is defined will determine how people choose to participate. If only those in formal roles are called leaders, others will not perceive themselves as leaders.

ACHIEVABLE AND SUSTAINABLE LEADERSHIP CAPACITY

When all those involved in the school community take responsibility for leading, the *leadership capacity* of an organization ensures the creation and sustainability of improvement. Leadership that is redefined as "the reciprocal processes of learning together in community" grows the leadership capacity of the entire organization.

Leadership capacity simply cannot be achieved with traditional notions of leadership. In Figure 2.1, note the dynamics or features of a high-leadership-capacity school (quadrant 4). Figure 2.2 describes traditional and constructivist leadership concepts as they apply to these features of leadership capacity.

Traditional leadership generally posits the notion of one or a few leaders who are driven by the formal leader's vision, which is in turn sold or marketed to the larger school community. Others may be involved in distributed or delegated leadership tasks, serving on teams, councils, or committees, though the final decisions usually reside with the principal. For the most part, accountability and assessment rely on standardized test scores, including the view that "inquiry" means examining test results. Staff training, technical coaching, and even teams may be focused narrowly on the implementation of a specific program, such as phonics,[2] or preparing for the tests. In such environments, staff members rarely evolve as mature, reflective human beings or take on the risks entailed in entrepreneurship. Teachers most

Teachers most often talk to principals about issues and feel isolated from or competitive with their colleagues. When these kinds of principals leave, the vacuum pulls the school backward, sacrificing any hope of sustainability.

Traditional Leadership Approaches and Actions	Constructivist Leadership Approaches and Actions
Principal's vision	Shared vision
Single/few "leaders" with formal authority	Multiple "leaders" including teachers, students, parents
"Non-leaders" provide input, advice, recommendations	Full participant engagement
Presentation of information, announcements of actions, policies	Dialogue for understanding and determining actions
Test data delivered to staff as information Test data used to make judgments about teacher and school effectiveness	Inquiry into questions of practice Multiple measures of performance used for assessing individual and group progress
Distributed, delegated tasks by formal leader	Fluid roles based on expertise, shared responsibilities
Implementation teams	Skilled teams with facilitators, dialogue, inquiry, action
Staff training	Professional development
Teachers communicate with principal regarding problems of practice	Teachers communicate with each other, as well as principal
Entrepreneurship discouraged; when it exists, it is behind closed doors	Entrepreneurship is encouraged as a generative of whole-school innovation
Technical coaching	Cognitive coaching

Figure 2.2   Leadership Capacity: Implications of Traditional and Constructivist Leadership

Source: Lambert, L. (2003). *Leadership capacity for lasting school improvement.* Alexandria, VA: Association for Supervision and Curriculum Development.

often talk to principals about issues and feel isolated from or competitive with their colleagues. When these kinds of principals leave, the vacuum pulls the school backward, sacrificing any hope of sustainability.

In the right-hand column of Figure 2.2, *constructivist leadership* frames the features of leadership capacity. A shared vision is co-constructed among multiple leaders who are fully engaged in leading the school. Acts of leadership are broadly constructed so that individuals envision a range of possible paths based on experience, disposition, and skills. For instance, listening well is an act of leadership; so are documenting school progress, coaching, planning, mentoring, and asking critical questions. Staff meetings, teams, and professional communities all use dialogue, inquiry, and action as the genesis of school improvement. Individuals and groups help each other to make sense of the process of schooling. Professional development, networking, and coaching seek to develop individuals through provoking their skills of thinking and reflection.

Test scores are only one form of assessment for effectiveness, part of an array of multiple measures of learning. Entrepreneurs have access to discretionary resources and school forums, so that individual passions have the power to generate multiple perspectives among community members. Figure 2.3 includes examples of coaching questions designed to enhance human development.

When principals lead in order to build leadership capacity, they lead for the day when they will no longer be around. Greg, principal at Lincoln High School (fictitious name) in San Francisco, observed that

> I'm trying to lead for *whenever I may not be here any longer*— by building both systems (through school design choices) and people's capacity for leadership, both of these focused on holding and progressing toward the vision. We have to strengthen both the vision and people's capacity to lead toward that vision.

Within this kind of leadership, teachers may enter into a state of self-organization. This state can be observed when the organization of a system spontaneously increases and becomes more complex; new roles and structures (e.g., webbed or nested communities, teaming) are formed by the participants. Initiating and self-responsible behaviors emerge that are not dependent on external direction. This emergence brings forth sustainable higher-level properties, e.g., a teacher leader or mentor becomes a better teacher. When self-organization occurs on the part of teachers, it marks a time when the principal can leave without regrets.

In a study of high-leadership-capacity schools (Lambert, 2006), my colleagues and I found three stages of development: (1) the

We are striving for language that invites the generation of new contexts or reframing of the group focus, opens up possibilities, and does not restrict answers to narrow categories or offer advice. These are grouped by the four reciprocal processes of constructivist leadership.

On Evoking Potential

What assumptions can I infer from . . .?
What do I think will happen or not happen as a result of holding these assumptions as true?
How long have I lived with this assumption?
When was it born, and under what circumstances? What has helped it grow up?
Have there been any significant turning points in its development? What is the life expectancy?
What information/evidence will I need to gather in order to challenge those assumptions?
How do I make sense of this?
What new actions may result from these understandings?
How might we . . .?
Why is that? When did we start doing it this way?
What led to . . .?
Tell us more about . . .
Explain what you mean by . . .

On Inquiring

What questions do we have?
What questions would be helpful to ask?
Based on our questions, what do we need to know?
What evidence would be useful? How can we find or discover this evidence?
When will we bring our evidence back to the group?
What will we do with this information?

On Sensemaking

Based on . . . what patterns do we see? What connections can we make?
How do we make sense of these? What meanings do they hold for us?
What conclusions can we draw?

On Reframing Action

Based on our findings, how do we need to change our practice? What changes do we need to make?
What is important for us in . . .?
What will it take to accomplish this?
What are we choosing to do?
How shall we proceed?
How might we reflect on our process? What have we learned?
How will you know when we are successful?

Figure 2.3   Constructivist Questions That Facilitate Dialogue

Source: Lambert, L., et al. (2002). *The constructivist leader* (2nd ed.). New York: Teachers College Press.

Instructive Stage, (2) the Transitional Stage, and (3) the High-Capacity Stage. The Instructive Stage refers to a period of organization, focusing, and establishing or initiating previously nonexistent structures and processes. The Transitional Stage is the process of letting go—releasing authority and control—while providing continuing support, guidance, and coaching. The High-Capacity Stage refers to developing the capacity in the organization and in individuals in ways that encourage teachers to assume more assertive roles. Through these processes, the role of the principal as the key player in the school decreases, while the roles of the teachers increase. Figure 2.4 describes the shifting behaviors and understandings in these stages.

The high-leadership-capacity district must also aim for broad-based, skillful participation in the work of leadership at all levels. In much the same way that schools can be organized, leadership in such districts is widely distributed among teachers, administrators, students, parents, and community members. A shared vision results in program coherence, and its meaning is continually reviewed and kept vibrant. Inquiry-based accountability systems inform decision making and practice at all levels. Accountability is reciprocal as well, meaning that feedback and critique are sought and used by both the district and the schools. Such reciprocity suggests high engagement among members of the educational communities, with a limited reliance on rules and regulations. Personnel are collaboratively selected and educated within a framework that integrates district and school responsibilities for professional development. Student achievement and development are high or steadily improving among all schools regardless of race, ethnicity, gender, or socioeconomic status.

The great challenge of the high-leadership-capacity district is, of course, sustainability. Sustainability involves the flexible capacity to self-organize, the art of the conversation, the depth and breadth of leadership participation, enculturation, and pacing. New York City's newest gimmick, A–F schools, violates the major tenets of capacity building. By ranking schools based on standardized test scores, a false standard is erected, one that results in public humiliation, competition, and low morale.

Sustainability involves the flexible capacity to self-organize, the art of the conversation, the depth and breadth of leadership participation, enculturation, and pacing.

Instructive Phase	Transitional Phase	High Leadership Capacity Phase
Principal as teacher, sponsor, director	*Principal as guide, coach*	*Principal as colleague, critical friend, mentor*
Personal attributes and behaviors: • Learns continually • Thinks strategically • Value/vision driven • Sets norms with staff • Supervises/ensures staff accountability • Convenes conversations • Honors history • Sponsors staff growth • Accepts responsibility • Breaks dependencies • Clarifies roles • Articulates strategies • Involves others in decision making • Creates safe, "holding" environment	Personal attributes and behaviors: • Learns—attends to epiphanies • Thinks strategically • Translates values into vision language • Lets go, provides support, and sticks around • Scaffolds with ideas and questions • Mediates roles • Develops structures that build reciprocal relationships • Coaches for instructional improvement	Personal attributes and behaviors: • Learns continually • Thinks strategically • Value/vision driven • Continues and expands behaviors initiated in earlier phases
Instructs staff (or arranges for instruction) in the following: • Collaboration, group processes, and teaming • Conversation and dialogue • Inquiry/data use • Trust building • Best instructional practices • Communication skills • Facilitation • Conflict resolution • Accountability	Guides staff to do the following: • Develop shared vision • Establish process observation of norms • Participate in leadership • Use inquiry • Question assumptions • Conduct constructivist conversations • Identify and solve problems • Surface/mediate conflict • Find resources (time, professional development, monies) • Plan	Participates with other members of the community to do the following: • Think strategically • Share concerns/ issues • Share decisions • Monitor and implement shared vision • Engage in reflective practices (reflection/ inquiry/dialogue/action) • Monitor norms and take self-corrective action • Build a culture of interdependency • Self-organize • Diversify and blend roles • Establish criteria for self-accountability

Instructive Phase	Transitional Phase	High Leadership Capacity Phase
Principal as teacher, sponsor, director	*Principal as guide, coach*	*Principal as colleague, critical friend, mentor*
		• Share authority and responsibility (dependent on expertise and interest, rather than role) • Plan for enculturation of new staff and succession
Uses formal authority to convene and maintain conversations, challenge complacency or incompetence, and make certain decisions	Uses formal authority to sustain conversations, insist on a professional development and inquiry agenda, mediate the demands of the district and state, and set reform pace	Uses formal authority to implement community decisions, mediate political pressures, work with less-than competent staff, and work on legal and reform challenges

Figure 2.4   Principal's Behaviors in Leadership Capacity Development

Source: The Educational Forum, Vol. 70, No. 3, Spring 2006, Kappa Delta Pi.

LEADERSHIP IMPLICATIONS FOR NCLB

No initiative in recent times challenges our thinking about leadership capacity and lasting leadership more dramatically than the No Child Left Behind Act (NCLB). This federal legislation seeks to improve the performance of all students primarily through the implementation of a nationwide testing program in Grades 3 through 8, with the intention of having every child performing at grade level by 2012.[3] Who could argue against school improvement, quality teachers, closing the achievement gap, evaluation, and accountability? And yet this program is based on the same premises as New York City's A–F program. Both approaches to the improvement of student performance are punitive, are built on the validity of test scores to measure learning and educator effectiveness, use public humiliation as motivation, and assume that educators could do better if they only chose to do so. In that regard, NCLB is fundamentally flawed, both in design and intent. Possibly worst of all, it may be the most problematic in the very schools it is designed to help.

- **NCLB is "dumbing down" the curriculum** as America teaches to the test, attempting to teach low-level skills in reading and math while *neglecting much of the content of learning and thinking:* the hard sciences, arts, social sciences, and technology. This is less true in already high-performing schools in affluent districts, where children do well on traditional tests anyway; it is the lower-performing schools that have been most victimized. Sheila Jordan, superintendent of schools in Alameda County, California, and Joan Davenport, professor at California State University, East Bay, have formed an alliance working with Harvard's Project Zero[4] as a means of improving cognition and critical thinking through the arts, one of the key domains neglected by NCLB.
- **Assessment and accountability are multifaceted, not just one-size-fits-all, multiple-choice tests.** States and schools need to be held to consistent, rigorous standards of accountability for school and student performance in all major subject areas. Such performance needs to be assessed among the same students over time (rather than just through yearly snapshots of students); each school needs to be credited for improvement or growth over time. This "growth model" approach is gaining momentum across the country, though the move to amend and reauthorize the law is slowed by the controversial "merit pay" rider (see Endnote). It is encouraging that Secretary of Education Margaret Spelling, as well as California Superintendent of Public Instruction Jack O'Connell, and a league of legislators are listening to the calls for distinguishing and acknowledging schools making progress toward goals.
- **Teachers are sacrificing good instruction for efficiency—all but giving up on learning experiences that foster creativity, self-reliance, initiative, and leadership.** Time on tests has drained time from relationships that offer a surefire way for teachers to reach students; time given to test trivialities has turned attention away from the professional learning *needed to close the achievement gap.* As First Lady Michelle Obama (2008) has noted, "NCLB is sucking the life out of our teachers."
- **NCLB requires all teachers to be fully credentialed in their subject areas. Quality teaching is more than an issue of credentialing.** Professional development opportunities are

absolutely necessary and should be funded. Experts in the field should be able to teach without a standard credential, e.g., under the law, a Nobel Laureate could not teach in a public school. Top-quality teachers need living salaries, or they turn to other professions that recognize their value.

- **NCLB calls for support providers and external evaluators who are often not qualified to provide relevant services. Parent support is an undervalued asset.** Less affluent schools, or those that do not have access to a support network, often find themselves without the guidance, parent involvement, coaching, and professional development that would lead to progress toward the most desirable of goals.

- **Most responses and legislative amendment proposals view the problems with NCLB as primarily ones of funding.** Underfunding poor policy leads to even deeper failure and disillusionment. However, a materially redesigned program should be created and then fully funded. The recognition of a flawed design helps to contradict the notion that its shortcomings reside primarily in implementation, e.g., inadequate resources, gaps in accountability planning, and support. It is not primarily an issue of funding, as it is with Head Start, which is driven by an excellent design.

However, even those who criticize NCLB may reluctantly admit that the initiative has succeeded in placing special education and bilingual education on the front burner. Catapulting these areas to the forefront of public attention may be more an act of desperation than compassion, since teachers in special education arenas have asked for decades that resources and students be integrated if America's schools are to succeed with all students. As Tom Ekno (personal communication, February 3, 2008), a special education teacher in Hawaii, points out, under NCLB the very goals of integration and mainstreaming are suffering as schools return to isolation and segregation in order to concentrate instruction. "NCLB ignores the instructional level of the child and requires that testing be done at grade level," Ekno explains. "Thereby instruction is often inappropriate, aimed at the tests rather than the needs of the student. I, like most educators, feel hamstrung by NCLB and find that most of the school day is devoted to appeasing NCLB at the expense of every child."

Yet, under NCLB, a school that does not succeed with all of its students will find the whole school condemned for not showing adequate yearly progress. Unless the entire school succeeds, everyone fails. Many otherwise high-performing schools and districts in affluent communities find themselves publicly embarrassed when their school is labeled as unsuccessful. These high-performing schools often boast of smart, experienced, qualified teachers and administrators; adequate resources; and supportive communities. So what's the problem? Why do these schools still fall short of succeeding with all students? Surely they have all the ingredients for success.

A critical issue rests with NCLB itself. Testing of students with a seventh-grade–level test when they may not yet be reading at the third-grade level, as well as a lack of acceptance of alternative measurements appropriate for students, may be at the core of the problem. Steady progress is often made but falls short of the artificial construct of uniform grade-level performance. Recognition of progress through the "growth model" could help to humanize some of the effects of NCLB.

However, responsibility for steady progress within frameworks of reasonable expectations rests with the school community and district: principals and district administrators, teachers and parents who can work together and share resources and talents, and therefore approach the issue as a body of learners and teachers. But working together is difficult. Anne Wilson of Boston College (personal communication, November 26, 2007) points out that even when teams are formed, conversations often focus almost exclusively on individual students and materials, and little progress is made toward the essential question: How do children's needs affect our practice? In other words, how do we reshape our practice to meet the needs of all students? What about our practice needs to change in order to get better results?

Just "telling" good teachers . . . to change practice has been historically unsuccessful. Change requires the insights derived from a culture of inquiry, which is the essence of leadership capacity.

Changing practice is at the heart of such reform, but just "telling" good teachers (or good doctors, businesspeople, farmers) to change practice has been historically unsuccessful. Change requires the insights derived from a culture of inquiry, which is the essence of leadership capacity. Individuals can arrive at their own decisions to alter practice through a process of skill-fully facilitated inquiry, involving the following:

- Professional development in facilitation, dialogue, and inquiry, including uses of all forms of data;
- A structure within which protocols of new practices are used on a regular basis (a part of which is regular meetings of inte-grated, cross-discipline teams with skilled facilitators—teacher leaders);
- Discretionary resources to enable new practices, including the collaborative piloting of innovations;
- A framework for action, with teacher leaders who assume multiple roles: communicating with other schools; asking challenging questions of each other, peer coaching, team teaching, curriculum and professional development designing and presenting, and advocacy at all levels; involvement in professional networks beyond the school (examples might include universities, the Association for Supervision and Curriculum Development, the National Staff Development Council, or the National Writing Project).

Such approaches build commitment and essential relationships, yet they still must occur within an aligned, focused district effort to achieve the goals that arise from these essential conversations. "Getting focused and staying focused is our greatest challenge and our greatest hope in education today," says Anne Conzemius (in press), "and it is nearly impossible within a larger system that, itself, cannot get focused" (p. 6).

Often answers, approaches, or processes just do not "occur" to us. They may be beyond the boundaries of our current practice or experience or culture. Unintended consequences, such as backing away from mainstreaming, go unnoticed. I prefer to think that good teachers and administrators do not think up good ideas and then reject them out of hand, even before they become vocalized. But, unfortunately, this does indeed happen. The failure to contribute provocative ideas is often derived from the fear of being ridiculed or thought less of—or, God forbid, having to take responsibility for implementing the idea. When seething cauldrons of ideas are triangulated—that is, three or more reform approaches are imple-mented together—these ideas emerge with energy and appeal.

Principals particularly need the understandings and skills discussed above. A thoughtful formal leader can help develop teacher leaders, establish the needed structures, disperse resources, and facilitate the engagement of the whole community. (It is more difficult for teacher leaders to develop their principals, but it can be done.) Therefore, a district serious about meeting the needs of all students must establish hiring practices designed to find and select those with the philosophy and potential to become leaders of inquiring communities. Such districts need to provide professional development and coaching to principals, as well as extend permission for them to challenge "business-as-usual" practices and say no to abusive mandates.

The above discussion began with the cases of high-performing schools that fall short of adequate yearly progress because of the performance of subgroups of students. Cases that begin with low-performing schools are even more dramatic, and decidedly more unfortunate. Many schools now spend more than half the day on basic skills; sacrificed are hard science, social science, the arts— and even recess!

Alyson Beahm (2007), from Noralto Elementary School in Sacramento, California, claims, "My school . . . is being torn apart, thanks to NCLB." More than 65 percent of the students in this underprivileged, high-poverty school are English language learners. This means that in the same year that children are learning English for the very first time, they must also pass a grade-level test. Although the school has made steady progress since 2002, the currently imposed goal of 35.2 percent cannot be met (and the goal will leap upward each year until 2014, when it is supposed to reach 100 percent). Beahm concludes, "This means that my school and thousands like it have 'failed.'. . . For us, this means that all non-tenured teachers will probably be fired by the end of this year and all permanent teachers could be 'involuntarily reassigned' elsewhere in the district. . . . How does this make sense? . . . The reality of NCLB is that it is sucking the joy out of education." It is little wonder that many believe NCLB to be an effort to bring an end to public schools by redirecting resources elsewhere.

The failure that haunts special-needs students, as well as English language learners, in many schools, haunts *most* students in low-performing schools. Too often, though not always, these schools are in poor, urban communities. Too often, they are populated almost exclusively by children of color. As noted above, in schools where performance is historically low, virtually all the instructional time is spent on those basic skills involved in the tests. *A new kind of gap has surfaced:* the gap between those who are learning science, history, technology, and the arts and those who are not. Consider the implications for our democracy, our economy, and our creative endeavors.

Hope lies in the realization that the same remedies described above for high-performing schools work equally well for low-performing schools. This understanding does not mean that schools and children are all alike. Clearly, the culture of poverty is different from the culture of affluence; financial resources and community support differ. But the culture of inquiry and professional learning serves as a framework on which to weave the fabric of reform in all schools.

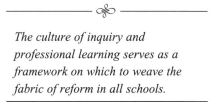

The culture of inquiry and professional learning serves as a framework on which to weave the fabric of reform in all schools.

The integration of talents and resources must be accompanied by the integration of curriculum and instruction. If reading and math are exclusive domains for learning in low-performing schools, then it is essential that the sciences and the arts be richly integrated within those curricular areas. Only then will programs have the depth and breadth that constitute true learning: achieving the knowledge and understandings that enable individuals and groups to derive meaning from life's experiences and take action to improve the multiple communities that constitute their worlds.

CONCLUSION

What is needed is a loom—a conceptual loom for leadership and a structural loom for leadership capacity. Edna St. Vincent Millay (1941) captured this urgency in "Huntsman, What Quarry?":

> Upon this gifted age, in its dark hour
>
> Rains from the sky a meteoric shower
>
> Of facts . . . they lie unquestioned, uncombined,
>
> Wisdom enough to leech us of our ill
>
> Is daily spun, but there exists no loom
>
> To weave it into fabric.

The "loom" is the schema or framework, such as leadership capacity, that envisions the dynamic that could be created in a system by broad participation with skillful leadership on everyone's part. This schema leads to high engagement and commitment by educators to the priorities set for student and adult learning. Yet when objectives are too constricted in response to exterior mandates, such as succeeding on a narrow test of basic skills, our tendency is to steer our work away from the natural course of change and teach to the test. Real changes evolve in a spiraling pattern from current practice, knowledge and understandings derived from data and observations of the children we serve, and continuing conversations. Children's passions and interests can lead us into unexpected realms, that is, unless our eyes are focused only on preset, narrow objectives.

In the small Italian town of Reggio Emilia lie early childhood schools that are widely recognized as the world's best. Built after World War II on a rich history of caring for children and the rights of women, this delightful medieval town set about developing the best schools possible.[5] Led by a visionary, Loris Malaguzzi, and an enthusiastic community, these schools, which insist that children are full citizens with unique voices, were founded on the principles of John Dewey, L. S. Vygotsky, Jean Piaget, Maria Montessori, and Jerome Bruner. As Malaguzzi imagined it, children have a hundred languages, and eyes that can "leap over the wall"—the wall that binds children to the routine, the ordinary, the noncreative . . . walls that are often understood by children and rejected before they enter fourth grade.

Reggio Children, the program's international center, works with alliances on six of the seven continents to establish a strong idea of childhood; promote study, research, and experimentation; advance professionalism and culture for teachers; and value the highlighting and documenting of children's and teachers' work within a community and a historical context. Each adult—and each student—is a leader of constructivist learning. The defining feature of their activities is the construction of reciprocal enrichment between what is known from experience and what is being learned. Research, the straining to know, is inseparable from professional development. No one teaches another "how to do school"; all seek to construct understandings and practice from dialogue and inquiry. Reggio Emilia has discovered a *loom,* a framework for schooling that has built the leadership capacity of the schools and community for sustainable greatness.

American schools as a whole do not work as well. As long as we consider just one weaver—the principal—and cannot portray the whole school community as composed of purposeful, inquiring leaders, our society will be relegated to settling for fragmented, simplistic recipes.

ENDNOTE

Although a seductive idea, merit pay paid to individual teachers has been historically unsuccessful. South Carolina, Kentucky, and Texas implemented merit pay and reaped the hazardous rewards: fragmented educational communities, competition rather than cooperation, pressure on administrators to award merit, and the woeful inadequacy of testing to determine merit. Merit pay that is awarded to schools rather than individuals, accompanied with the discretion for distribution, holds more promise, for its effect can be communal cohesiveness rather than divisiveness. Incentive pay for challenging teaching venues or stipends for additional roles have potential for stimulating improvement as well, if carefully planned so that those on the outside looking in do not feel disengaged.

NOTES

1. Jim Collins (2007) has studied sustainability organizations with important results, finding "Level 5" leaders to have certain qualities such as personal humility and professional will.

2. Such approaches to improvement assume that the solution is known before fully understanding the problem. Most often, these "remedies" are imported from the outside.

3. Carl Cohn (2007), superintendent of the San Diego schools, laments, "I believe there is a place where no child is left behind, where all children achieve grade-level proficiency, and there is no achievement gap. It is called Heaven."

4. Project Zero is designed to create communities of reflective, independent learners; to enhance deep understanding within disciplines; and to promote critical and creative thinking.

5. All young children who live within this community may attend these exceptional schools. Consequently, Reggio Emilia has one of the highest birthrates in Europe. Bologna, just 45 minutes away (and indeed, the rest of Italy), has one of the lowest birthrates in Europe.

References

Beahm, A. (2007, December 2). Quality education gets lost in translation. *San Francisco Chronicle.*

Cohn, C. (2007, April). NCLB. *Education Week.*

Collins, J. (2007). Level 5 leadership. *Jossey-Bass reader on educational leadership* (2nd ed.). San Francisco: Jossey-Bass.

Conzemius, A. (in press). Getting S.M.A.R.T. about reform. *School Administrator.*

Conzemius, A., & O'Neill, J. (2001). *Shared responsibility for student learning.* Alexandria, VA: Association for Supervision and Curriculum Development.

Lambert, L. (2003). *Leadership capacity for lasting school improvement.* Alexandria, VA: Association for Supervision and Curriculum Development.

Lambert, L. (2006, Spring). Lasting leadership: A study of leadership capacity in schools. *Educational Forum.*

Lambert, L., Walker, D., Zimmerman, D., Cooper, J., Lambert, M., Gardner, M., & Szabo, M. (2002). *The constructivist leader* (2nd ed.). New York: Teachers College Press.

Millay, E. S. (1941). *Collected sonnets.* New York: Harper & Row.

Obama, M. (2008, February 3). Speech given at a political rally at UCLA.

Senge, P., Scharmer, C. O., Jaworski, J., & Flowers, B. S. (2004). *Presence: Human purpose and the field of the future.* New York: Currency, Doubleday.

CHAPTER THREE

THE MORAL IMPERATIVE REVISITED

Achieving Large-Scale Reform

MICHAEL FULLAN

I n 2003 I published *The Moral Imperative of School Leadership,* emphasizing that the concept "moral imperative" has replaced the overused concept of vision. Moral imperative implied greater gusto and a sense of urgency. It is about serving the needs of each and every student, which means that it is especially about "raising the bar and closing the gap." Any group in society that lags behind deserves added attention.

I then suggested that the school principal is especially well placed to focus on the moral imperative. This new role was demanding, I wrote, because it involves two levels within the school: making a difference in lives of individuals (a student, a teacher, a parent), and in the school as a whole (new collaborative cultures in which the performance of the whole school would be enhanced).

I also described two more levels, external to the school. Level 3 concerned networks or clusters of schools wherein individual principals learned from other schools, while contributing to the development of other schools in the network. The fourth level involved society as a whole. Principals, I suggested, needed to drill down within their own schools, but they also needed to be plugged into the larger picture. They needed to realize that improvements in their own schools are part and parcel of societal development.

———— ✌ ————

Moral purpose is no longer confined to this or that individual act, but rather is a quality of the entire organization or system.

The moral imperative signaled that moral purpose is no longer confined to this or that individual act, but rather is a quality of the entire organization or system. With this in mind, it is worth noting that in the 5 years since publication of *The Moral Imperative of School Leadership,* the most significant accomplishment has been the development and flourishing of powerful and specific strategies necessary to bring the moral imperative into being on a larger scale. In this chapter, I'll first take the case of Ontario, Canada, as a comprehensive example of this phenomenon. Second, I'll identify and discuss the "theory of action" that underpins the new strategies being used—strategies that enable us to address the moral imperative across whole systems to the benefit of all. I call this theory of action the Six Secrets of Change (Fullan, 2008a).

THE ONTARIO CASE: 2003–2007

Since 2003 I have served as Special Adviser in Education to the Premier of Ontario following the government's election in October of that year. Fresh from writing *The Moral Imperative,* I was charged with seeing what could be done to substantially improve the entire public school system in Ontario—2 million students, 72 school districts, 4,000 elementary schools, and 900 secondary schools.

The Premier of Ontario, Dalton McGuinty, declared that literacy and numeracy would be the top priority; a year later he added high school graduation as a third priority. In the previous 5 years, the province had stagnated or flatlined on all three measures; that is, no improvements had been made in literacy, numeracy, or high school graduation from 1998–2003.

Many jurisdictions use the rhetoric of moral purpose—No Child Left Behind (NCLB) being a prime example. The telling point is whether or not they have an explicit, powerful set of strategies to go along with it. Moral purpose is merely an empty declaration without a strategy to get there.

In this chapter, I argue that moral purpose without a strategy is an exercise in futility. The task is not only to focus on strategy, but also to become increasingly more specific in identifying, retaining, and building on high-yield strategies that produce results.

In Ontario we started with the following strategic components:

- Ambitious, measurable goals publicly announced;
- A focus on capacity building;
- Identification and spread of best practices;
- Transparency of results linked to nonjudgmental intervention; and
- Communication, communication, communication.

Setting a small number of ambitious, high-leverage goals is crucial. Jurisdictions that try to do everything at once—when everything is made an equal priority—never seem to excel at any of them. For us, literacy, numeracy, and high school graduation represented core priorities around which to rally resources and action. Literacy and numeracy are deeply defined to include many of the so-called 21st-century skills such as interpretation, reasoning, communication, expression, problem solving, and so on. High school graduation means that high schools must engage in innovation in order to make school engaging and relevant to students who might otherwise drop out.

In Ontario an independent agency called the Education, Quality, and Accountability Office (EQAO) conducts annual assessments on reading, writing, and math in Grades 3 and 6, and on a Grade 10 literacy test as well as the rates of high school graduation. A fairly high level of proficiency is required to meet the provincial standard, which is set at a 70 percent passing rate for individuals. By focusing on the starting point (54 percent for literacy and numeracy), and setting new targets (75 percent), the spotlight was focused on a measurable outcome. (By 2007 the attainment rate for both literacy and numeracy had increased to 64 percent.) Similarly, high school graduation rates were at 69 percent in 2003, with a target of 85 percent by 2010. (As of 2007, the graduation rate had risen to 75 percent.)

There is little point in having targets if there is no accompanying strategy to reach the targets. One of the most powerful sets of strategies consists of capacity building. Capacity concerns new knowledge, skills, and competencies known to relate to increased performance. We divide these capacities into two components: (1) instructional and (2) management of change. Instructional competencies pertain to effective teaching practices in literacy and numeracy, as well as practices that engage students in their own learning. Management of change strategies involve competencies related to developing collaborative cultures, the pace of change, handling resistance, and dealing with the always-present multitude of external demands.

There is little point in having targets if there is no accompanying strategy to reach the targets.

In Ontario we established a new unit within the province's Ministry of Education called the Literacy and Numeracy Secretariat (LNS). The LNS consists of approximately 100 people organized into seven teams. Six of the teams are regional; they work with 10 or 11 districts each, helping them to focus on goals, capacities, assessment, and intervention. The seventh team, which is responsible for research and inquiry, conducts studies on the state of implementation, lessons learned, and so forth. The general idea is to triangulate goals, implementation, and assessment of results and best practice.

A third component of the strategy just referred is to continually identify and spread effective practices, whether they be at the classroom level, schoolwide, or districtwide. The flow of best knowledge is crucial in any change effort, and one must have an explicit strategy to capture and make available this knowledge as it is generated.

The flow of best knowledge is crucial in any change effort, and one must have an explicit strategy to capture and make available this knowledge as it is generated.

The fourth strategic component concerns the power of data. Governments typically make one or more of the following mistakes when it comes to data: they generate too much data (information overload), they make it available too late or in an unusable format, or they do not work on developing strategies to use the data.

The use of data for improvement is one of the highest-yield strategies we know about, but it requires great care and sophistication. One aspect of the strategic use of data is to build up the capacity of teachers and teacher leaders (coaches, mentors, principals) to integrate "assessment for learning" techniques into the classroom. A second component is to establish a solid, timely database for all schools. For example, we created a data set called "Statistical Neighbors." The database includes just six measures for all 4,000 elementary schools: reading, writing, and math for Grades 3 and 6. The schools are grouped according to one of four categories based on degree of poverty or challenge facing the school (hence the label "statistical neighbors").

There are several key ground rules and assumptions involved in using the Statistical Neighbors database. First, it is used to set and track progress annually. From the individual school's perspective, we encourage each school to (1) compare itself with itself, i.e., with its own starting point; (2) compare itself with other schools in similar circumstances (the apples-to-apples comparison); and (3) compare itself with an overall standard (such as how the whole system is doing).

For systemwide use, there are three critical assumptions and one major strategy. We do not condone "league tables" (wherein schools are ranked independently of context), because this leads to unfair comparisons—and endless debate. We do not overly interpret 1 year's results at a time, preferring 3-year windows that allow anyone to see if a school is moving upward, declining, or flatlining. We base any intervention on capacity building, avoiding stigmatized judgment.

In the matter of low-performing schools, we have developed an intervention strategy based on capacity building called the Ontario Focused Intervention Program (OFIP). There are currently 1,100 (of the 4,000) elementary schools involved in OFIP. Of these, 400 are the lowest-performing schools; the other 700 are schools with flatlined performance over the 3 years. (They may have a decent average score but are stagnant as schools.)

The LNS works out a capacity-building strategy with each of the schools and its district. Strategies are specific as to instruction, teachers working with coaches, and so forth. We have been careful to take the judgment out of OFIP—schools do not feel stigmatized, a crucial ingredient when it comes to motivation. The strategy seems to work; last year OFIP schools improved on the average 10 percentage points more than the rest of the provincial schools in EQAO assessments of literacy and numeracy.

The final large component of our strategy is communication, communication, communication. Traditionally, governments communicate about their vision (goals), but not about their strategies. We have found that making the "theory of action" explicit plays an important role in focusing people's efforts on the "how-to's"—on capacity building, monitoring, and intervention. Communication must also be continuous and two-way. People must be constantly reminded about and engaged in the strategies-in-action. In so doing, leaders at all levels need to seek and listen to feedback on the goals, quality of implementation, and meaning of results.

OUTCOMES

Taken together, these five central components—ambitious goals, focus on capacity building, spread of effective practices, the power of data, and communication—make a difference. The percentage of proficient students in literacy and numeracy in Grades 3 and 6 has increased by 10 percentage points over 4 years; the percentage of students graduating from high school has gone up 6 percentage points. Teacher and principal morale has also improved. As one indirect indication of improved morale, prior to the strategy some 30 percent of beginning teachers had left the profession by their fourth year of teaching; that figure is currently running at less than 10 percent.

NEXT STEPS

By integrating moral purpose with strategies to get there, the whole system benefits. The provincial government was reelected for a second 4-year term (2007–2011) and has mapped out a deeper agenda based on its first-term success (Ontario Ministry of Education, 2008). A core part of this agenda involves going deeper into both literacy and numeracy. The strategies are now more specific, more precise, and more powerful; they focus increasingly on the higher-order performance skills. Second, key linkages are being established with other connected priorities receiving emphasis—namely, early childhood development, the arts, citizenship education, teacher education, leadership development, and parent engagement. Third, we have made more specific a basic goal that previously was only implied: to increase the public's confidence in the public education system. Now that this goal has been named, strategies of engagement are being launched and measures of public satisfaction are being employed.

THE SIX SECRETS OF CHANGE

Although I have used only one case to illustrate the key point that the moral imperative must play itself out as an integral part of whole-system improvement, with accompanying explicit strategies, these core ideas are evident in much of our work around the world. More and more countries are committing themselves and their schools to raising the bar and closing the gap, to capacity building, and to focusing on results and tracking progress both internally and internationally.

In my most recent book, *The Six Secrets of Change,* I tested the underlying theory of action against evidence in the business literature as well as within the education sector. The results are confirmatory. I expressed the findings in the language of six "secrets" (secrets in the sense that they have deep meanings that must be grasped; see Figure 3.1).

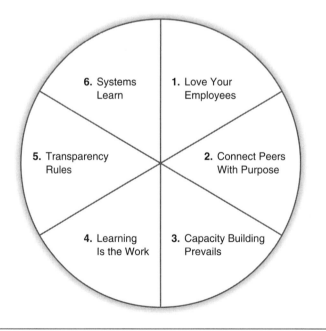

Figure 3.1   The Six Secrets of Change

Source: Fullan, M. (2008a). *The six secrets of change: What the best leaders do to help their organizations survive and thrive.* San Francisco: Jossey-Bass. Reprinted with permission of John Wiley & Sons, Inc.

The secrets (see Figure 3.1) work in combination, bringing out the best in all of us, providing checks and balances for the worst tendencies. For example, transparency can sometimes be misused to name and shame low performers, but when combined with loving your employees and capacity building, it works positively—and is essential.

In the rest of this chapter, I elaborate briefly on each of the six secrets. I call the entire set of secrets "Have theory, will travel," because if you understand the secrets in action it enables you to formulate and carry out powerful strategies that produce deep and sustained results. In explaining the secrets, I use generic language (employees, customers, etc.) to signify that these ideas apply to all organizations. These secrets have been derived from our experiences in bringing about large-scale reform, and have been tested against the education and business literature dealing with deep successful change (see Fullan, 2008a).

In brief, the secrets are

1. *Love your employees as much as your customers.* If you build your organization by focusing on your customers without the same careful commitment to your employees, you won't succeed for long. We have all seen the opposite, of course: the organization that seems to run for the benefit of the employees, with the customer perceived as an intrusion. Neither will do. There is powerful evidence that investing in your employees in the right way can be enormously profitable. The key is enabling employees to learn continuously and to find meaning in their work and in their relationship to coworkers and to the organization as a whole.

> *The key is enabling employees to learn continuously and to find meaning in their work and in their relationship to coworkers and to the organization as a whole.*

Moreover, it is clear that the most effective organizations cast their moral net widely. For example, Sisodia, Wolfe, and Sheth (2007), in their study of 28 companies selected for their "humanistic purpose," found that these firms held in equally high regard the following: employees, customers, investors or shareholders, partners (suppliers), and society. All five groups were consciously valued in the firms' actions. In terms of performance, these companies outperformed the Standard and Poor's index average by 1,026 percent over a 10-year period! They also outperformed Jim Collins's 11 so-called great companies, which only outperformed the average by 331 percent—less than a third of the performance of the humanistic companies. And yes, "contribution to society" was explicitly valued by these companies, which included Toyota, Southwest Airlines, Starbucks, Whole Foods, Costco, and 23 others.

2. *Connect peers with purpose.* All large-scale reform efforts in any public or private sector face the too tight/too loose dilemma. If you want whole-system reform, you need to focus and tighten the requirements, but if you go too far in that direction, people feel constrained and rebel. On the other hand, local people need to be empowered. So if you devolve power and resources to local entities—the "Let a thousand flowers bloom" approach—you get massively uneven results. (A thousand flowers do not in fact bloom, and those that do are not perennial!) The solution to this dilemma comes from the top, but not directly. It comes from leaders who embed strategies that foster continuous, purposeful peer interaction. The social glue of simultaneous tight-loose systems occurs not when rank-and-file workers fall in love with the hierarchy, but rather when they fall in love with their peers.

Purposeful peer interaction achieves what I call the we-we factor. In collaborative schools, for example, individual teachers stop focusing on "my students" only and start valuing *all* students in the school. When schools interact in a network, individual principals stop focusing on "my school" only and start being concerned with the success of all schools in the network. And so on. What causes effectiveness in these situations is (1) the spread of knowledge and effective practices, and (2) an enlarged sense of identity and commitment—the latter being none other than moral purpose writ large.

3. *Capacity building trumps judgmentalism.* Capacity building is when leaders invest in the development of individual and collaborative efficacy of a whole group or system in order to accomplish significant improvements. In particular, capacity consists of new competencies, new resources (time, ideas, expertise), and new motivation.

Many theories of action use fear and punitive accountability. The latter achieves only short-term and fleeting results at best. The opposite—nonjudgmentalism—does not mean that you avoid identifying things as effective or ineffective. Rather, it means that you do not do so pejoratively. Put another way, there are better ways of instilling fear than through negative judgment, for example, by combining transparency and peer interaction. Pejorative judgments certainly have their place, as when someone is abusive or engaged in criminal and fraudulent acts, but as motivators they should be used sparingly. The main gains will come from the six secrets in concert—none of which contains blatant judgmentalism.

Our success, for example, in the Ontario Focused Intervention Partnership in turning around lower-performing schools is partly due to the new capacities we help instill, but also because of the "attitude" we bring to the strategies. Take away negative judgment at the beginning, and you clear away a lot of the motivational problems. You still, as I have said, identify ineffective practices in order to correct them, and you sometimes eventually must take strong action, but a large part of the success involves getting started *positively* on making improvements.

4. *Learning is the job.* One of our Australian colleagues wrote an article with the wonderful title "Professional Development: A Great Way to Avoid Change" (Cole, 2004). In other words, there is far too much going to workshops, taking short courses, and the like, and far too little learning while doing the work. Obviously, I favor external-to-the-job learning, but if it is not in balance with, and in concert with, learning in the setting where you work, it will end up being superficial. Effective organizations see working and learning to work better as one and the same.

Richard Elmore (2004) has made this very observation in noting that successful reform involves "learning in context" or "learning in the setting in which you work." Alas, he says, very few school cultures provide continuous and daily opportunities to learn in this way. In our "breakthrough" model (how to get full success in teaching literacy, for example), we claimed that this is not possible unless each and every teacher is learning every day, individually and collectively (Fullan, Hill, & Crévola, 2006).

5. *Transparency rules.* By transparency, I mean clear and continuous display of results, and clear and continuous access to practice (what is being done to get the results). Transparency can be abused, such as when results are used punitively, but there is no way that continuous improvement can occur without constant transparency fueled by good data. When transparency is practiced in combination with the other five secrets, the gains far outweigh the costs. Besides, transparency is here to stay in the hyper-connected world of the 21st century. We have found that when transparency is well positioned, it creates an aura of "positive pressure"—pressure that is experienced as fair and reasonable, pressure that is actionable

in that it points to solutions, and pressure that at the end of the day is inescapable.

While transparency can have its downfalls (as when results are used to punish), on balance it is one of the most powerful high-yield strategies we know. Assessment for learning, closely linked to instructional improvements, makes huge differences in student learning, but we are still stymied in many cases by teachers who teach in isolation. The "de-privatization" of teaching—that is, when teachers find it normal and desirable to view each other's teaching and to work with coaches and mentors to engage in continuous improvement—remains one of the last frontiers of school improvement. De-privatization is one of the most important outcomes "worth fighting for" (Fullan, 2008b).

6. *Systems learn.* Systems themselves can learn on a continuous basis. The synergistic result of the previous five secrets is tantamount to establishing a system that learns from itself. Two dominant change forces are unleashed and constantly cultivated: knowledge and commitment. People learn new things all the time, and their broader knowledge can lead to heightened motivation and commitment.

There are two components to this secret. One involves developing collaborative cultures in which leaders not only focus on the moral imperative but do so in a way that produces other leaders as they go—the so-called distributive leadership. This builds in renewal as you go.

The other feature is fostering and developing leaders who are simultaneously confident and humble in the face of complexity. This has been a consistent finding in the literature. I maintain that cultivating the previous five secrets in action develops such leaders.

In conclusion, the moral imperative is not just rhetoric, even if sincerely meant. It must be combined with powerful strategies to make it a reality in practice. When this happens, you not only accomplish more, but moral purpose also becomes much more meaningful in the hearts and minds of all educators and even the public. It comes to have an additional life of its own, further powering it forward. The six secrets of change embedded with a clear moral purpose can be unstoppable. We have never been in a better position to act on this knowledge, and there has never been a time when informed moral action is more needed for the survival of society.

The six secrets of change embedded with a clear moral purpose can be unstoppable.

REFERENCES

Cole, P. (2004). *Professional development: A great way to avoid change.* Melbourne, Australia: Centre for Strategic Change.

Elmore, R. (2004). *School reform from the inside out.* Cambridge, MA: Cambridge University Press.

Fullan, M. (2003). *The moral imperative of school leadership.* Thousand Oaks, CA: Corwin.

Fullan, M. (2008a). *The six secrets of change.* San Francisco: Jossey-Bass.

Fullan, M. (2008b). *What's worth fighting for in the principalship?* (2nd ed.). New York: Teachers College Press; Toronto, Canada: Ontario Principals' Council.

Fullan, M., Hill, P., & Crévola, C. (2006). *Breakthrough.* Thousand Oaks, CA: Corwin; Toronto, Canada: Ontario Principals' Council.

Ontario Ministry of Education. (2008). *Energizing Ontario education.* Toronto, Canada: Author.

Sisodia, R., Wolfe, D., & Sheth, J. (2007). *Firms of endearment.* Upper Saddle River, NJ: Wharton School Publishing.

CHAPTER FOUR

LEADERSHIP FOR MORTALS

Developing and Sustaining
Leaders of Learning[1]

DEAN FINK

Many years ago a riotous song called "Jake the Peg," by an Australian entertainer named Rolf Harris, became internationally popular. Jake was a three-legged man who had difficulty knowing which leg to use at any given moment and inevitably fell on his face. Leaders in the first decade of the 21st century are like Jake the Peg. They have one leg in Traditional Public Administration, since most still work in hierarchical bureaucracies; one leg in New Public Management as they struggle with state curricula, standardized testing, and site-based management; and a third leg in Professional Learning Communities as they work to refocus their schools and local communities on students' learning.

THE CHALLENGE

The first of the three "legs," Traditional Public Administration (TPA), describes the bureaucratized, hierarchical organizations that have prevailed for decades and continue to predominate in many educational jurisdictions around the world. Substantive change within TPA has inevitably foundered on bureaucratic inertia, political timidity, community nostalgia, and the resistance of teachers. The organizational structures of most schools around the world are still fundamentally unchanged since the beginning of the century—the 20th century, that is. They are for the most part hierarchical, bureaucratized, and balkanized (Hargreaves, 1994).

The organizational structures of most schools around the world are still fundamentally unchanged since the beginning of the century—the 20th century, that is.

While the historical structures have remained intact, recent policy efforts by governments (usually described as "New Public Management") have attempted to focus schools' efforts on results, as opposed to inputs and processes, through the use of market forces, standardized high-stakes testing, and stringent curriculum requirements. These policies, the second "leg," have placed unique pressures on leaders, and in the process have undermined educational leadership and replaced it with a form of instrumental managerialism that undercuts the very purposes of schools. While so-called New Public Management can claim short-term gains, serious questions remain as to its efficacy in sustaining important changes over time (Nichols & Berliner, 2007).

As a result, a third form of public policy dialogue, the third "leg," which focuses on organizations as "professional learning communities," has emerged. A learning community aims to enhance the learning of all participants in an organization as a way of advancing and sustaining its purposes (Hargreaves & Fink, 2006; Stoll, Fink, & Earl, 2003; Stoll & Seashore Louis, 2007). Moving schools in this direction will require leaders who are "leaders of learning," who can engage their colleagues in a shared commitment to improve the learning opportunities for all students. For contemporary leaders, who still work within traditional bureaucracies, dealing with the fallout from New Public Management while developing their schools as learning communities creates unprecedented but not impossible difficulties. The challenge for a leader in education today is to learn how to balance on all three legs while simultaneously leading his or her school to become a learning community. This challenge of the "three-legged man" is beyond the capabilities of any one person, regardless of how heroic, charismatic, or brilliant he or she may be.

Rather than looking at school leaders as individuals, we need to look at school leadership as a pervasive force across schools and school districts. We need also to examine how dedicated "mortals" can work together to shape school and district leadership in ways that ensure challenging, creative learning experiences for all students. In thinking about developing and sustaining leadership that real people can accomplish, there are certain aspects of leadership that must never change, and other aspects that must change as circumstances dictate. For the purpose of this chapter, I deal with two features of what I have called "leadership for mortals" that must never change: absolute *commitment* to student learning, and a set of life-affirming *values* that sustain leaders through good times and bad. I also examine two facets of leadership that should always change and evolve and grow: the *learnings* required to be leaders of learning, and the intellectual and emotional *qualities* that all potential leaders possess that must be developed and sustained. They are part of a larger model that is diagrammed in Figure 4.1 and developed in detail elsewhere (Fink, 2005).[2]

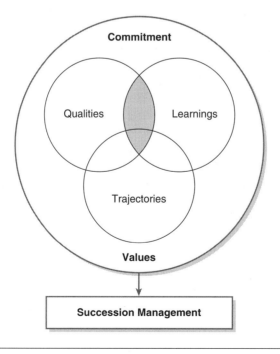

Figure 4.1

COMMITMENT

In the past decade, I have had the good fortune to visit with school leaders in over 30 different countries who are doing a magnificent job of leading learning for all their students in far more challenging conditions than I ever experienced in my own leadership career. There is Jane in Australia, for example, who heads up one of the most challenging schools in New South Wales with quiet dignity, passion, and effectiveness. Then there is Allan, who has turned a gang-ridden school in the heart of the most troubled section of Belfast into an oasis of safety and learning. Elena, in Piscu, Romania, is principal of a small school in a preindustrial village; she inspires her staff daily to achieve great things with children, with virtually no support from the government and with infrequent paychecks. Then there is Charmaine in Ontario, who refuses to adopt quick-fix remedies for the language problems of her racially and ethnically diverse school. She has challenged her staff to promote literacy across the curriculum, and in the process raised her school's achievement on the provincial high-stakes literacy test from below the median to second place in her very large school district—ahead of all but one of the middle-class schools in the leafy suburbs.

Nice stories, yes, but what's the point? The point is that leaders of learning come in all shapes and sizes, genders, races, religions, backgrounds, and contexts. These are not heroes, or even people uniquely blessed with leadership abilities (though they have these capacities in abundance). Instead, they are ordinary people who—through extraordinary commitment, effort, and determination—have become extraordinary, and have made the people around them exceptional. Educational leadership is more art than science; it is more about character than technique; it is more about inspiration than charisma; it is more about leading students' and teachers' learning than about the management of things. Such leaders not only understand the challenges of their contexts, and commit totally to ensuring such learning for all their students; they also possess a

Leaders of learning are ordinary people who—through extraordinary commitment, effort, and determination—have become extraordinary, and have made the people around them exceptional.

philosophy, a mind-set, a "story," a "stance," a value system that guides all of their leadership activities.

VALUES

Rudy Giuliani, mayor of New York City at the time of the Twin Towers disaster, said, "Great leaders lead by ideas" (2002, p. 170). I would amend that slightly: "Great leaders lead by *great* ideas." Leadership begins with a story (Gardner, 1996), a philosophy, a set of core values, a point of view, an educational "stance" that passionately motivates a leader and engages his or her followers.

In a previous publication (Stoll & Fink, 1996), Louise Stoll and I have carved out our "story" around a "great" idea called *invitational leadership.* An invitation is "a summary description of messages, formal and informal, verbal and non-verbal, continuously transmitted to others to inform them that they are able, worthwhile, and responsible" (Purkey & Novak, 1984, p. 5). From this definition of an "invitation," we went on to state that invitational leadership "is about communicating invitational messages to individuals and groups in order to build and act on a shared and evolving vision of enhanced educational experiences for all pupils" (Stoll & Fink, 1996, p. 106). As this definition suggests, our "story" is not so much a definitive leadership style that competes with academically defined leadership approaches, but rather a values-based approach to leadership and life that promotes life-affirming policies and practices in schools and school districts and is predicated on a set of interrelated, interconnected values—trust, respect, optimism, and intentionality—that provide a foundation or touchstone for leaders in good times and in bad.

Trust. The foundation of a civil society is trust. Can we trust our political leaders, our business community, our educators, the press? The erosion of trust can have serious consequences. The Enron and MCI scandals in the United States seriously undermined trust in the economic system and particularly trust in large, multinational corporations. Even before the Enron fiasco, in fact, only 47 percent of the employees surveyed in American companies believed that their own corporate leaders were people of integrity. Moreover, 58 percent of these employees thought that top-level executives were out for themselves, and only 33 percent thought that top executives were interested in advancing the interests of their organizations (Mintzberg, 2004). President Bill Clinton's deceptions about his sexual activities in the 1990s, as well as the more recent misinformation surrounding the decisions of the United States and Britain to invade Iraq, have seriously shaken societal trust in politicians and the intelligence communities in both countries. The political partisanship of some television news channels and print media has produced skepticism and cynicism, especially among younger people. The terrible cases of the abuse of trusting children by clerics have eroded trust in the most sacred of our institutions.

As Kouzes and Posner (2003) report, in America "the cynics are winning. The regard for leaders from all organized groups—politics, government, business, labor, and the church—is so low that they are no longer paid much heed. And lack of confidence has led people to be less willing to participate in the struggle to improve" (p. 5). It is therefore ironic that governments intent on educational improvement throughout the Western world, with the assistance of a compliant press, have systemically attempted to undermine the bonds of trust between schools and their communities. For example, the Chief Inspector of Education in the United Kingdom under both Prime Ministers John Major and Tony Blair habitually named and blamed teachers for every real and imagined ill in the system. If his efforts were intended to motivate, his strategy backfired. "You can't make people winners by calling them losers" (Williams, 2002, p. 88). When relationships go wrong, the place to start rebuilding is in the area of trust, which is not always easy. Rebuilding that bond of trust with teachers and parents has proven to be a very difficult task for the British government.

"Honesty is absolutely essential to leadership. If people are going to follow someone willingly, whether it is into battle or into the boardroom, they want to assure themselves that the person is worthy of trust" (Kouzes & Posner, 2003, p. 253). In their study of the characteristics of America's most admired leaders, Kouzes and Posner reported that 83 percent of their respondents rated honesty as the most important quality for business leaders (p. 253). There is ample evidence (Louis & Kruse, 1996; Malloy, 1998; Meier, 1995; Newman & Associates, 1996) that social trust is a key ingredient for school improvement and that the only way to engender trust is to be absolutely trustworthy. Personal integrity is absolutely crucial to leadership; it doesn't require superhuman qualities to achieve, just courage and determination. Trusting relationships are also respectful relationships.

Respect. We all need to be acknowledged as the unique people we are—to be viewed as able, valuable, responsible human beings, not just cogs in a machine or numbers to be processed or "human capital." We all need invitations. Unfortunately, our hurried society has little time to listen to us or even acknowledge our uniqueness and humanity. The pressures of high-stakes tests, aggressive parents, misbehaving students, and zealous politicians can get in the way of showing respect to colleagues, students, and other key stakeholders.

> *We all need to be acknowledged as the unique people we are—to be viewed as able, valuable, responsible human beings, not just cogs in a machine or numbers to be processed or "human capital." We all need invitations.*

Educators are not alone in feeling harried. In their study of what followers look for in their leaders in the business community, Kouzes and Posner (2003) report that the quality that followers demand of their leaders that has shown the most significant increase from the 1980s to the 1990s is supportiveness: people "require more understanding and help from their leaders" (p. 19). Perhaps the best way to show respect is to follow Stephen Covey's (1989) advice—to seek first to understand and then to be understood. William Glasser (1997) says we have four basic needs: to care and feel cared for, to have some power over our circumstances, to have hope for the future, and to have fun (p. 596). Respect involves caring and empowerment; optimism incorporates hope and fun.

Optimism. Giuliani states in his book *Leadership* (2002),

> It's up to the leader to instill confidence, to believe in his judgment, and in people even when they no longer believe in themselves. Sometimes the optimism of the leader is grounded in something only he knows—the situation isn't as dire as people think for reasons that will eventually become clear. But sometimes the leader has to be optimistic simply because if he isn't no one else will be. And you have to at least fight back no matter how daunting the odds. (p. 296)

Kouzes and Posner (2003) report that, after honesty, "forward-looking" leadership is what people look for in their leaders. They want to know their leaders have a vision, a sense of direction, and a destination. The teacher you worshipped, the principal you admired, the university professor you tried to emulate—all responded either explicitly or implicitly to your need to get answers to such conscious or unconscious questions as, Do you know where you're going? Is it a trip worth taking? Am I invited to go along? They responded to your hopes at the time, and quieted your fears. They made the journey memorable and enjoyable, if not outright fun.

Sergiovanni (2004) asserts that placing "hope at the center of our school community provides encouragement and promotes clear thinking and informed action, giving us the leverage we need to close the achievement gap and solve other intractable problems" (p. 33). However, he discriminates between hope that is grounded in realism and wishful thinking that takes no deliberate action to make wishes come true. The key to hopeful or optimistic leadership, therefore, is to develop intentionally a systematic approach to school improvement. It is intentionality, the fourth of the invitational values or principles, that gives trust, respect, and optimism their purpose and direction.

Intentionality. Intentionality is the engine that engages invitational leaders and their colleagues in developing and sustaining actionable plans that promote student learning within a values-based framework. Without intentionality, stated values become rather hollow, or worse. For example, Jeffrey Skillings, the disgraced former head of Enron, described his job as "doing God's work." His successor, Ken Lay, who before his untimely death was indicted for various breaches of trust, stated that "one of the most satisfying things in life is to create a high moral and ethical environment in which every individual is allowed and encouraged to realize that God-given potential" (Csikszentmihalyi, 2004). These are wonderful sentiments, to be sure, but more than a bit hypocritical when actions do not support them.

A THEORY OF EVERYTHING

From an educational leadership perspective, an invitational framework provides a "theory of action" based on four unchanging core premises:

1. Education is a cooperative, collaborative activity in which process is as important as product.

2. People are able, valuable, and responsible and should be treated accordingly.

3. People possess untapped potential in all areas of human endeavor.

4. Human potential can best be realized by creating a total school culture specifically designed to invite development, and by people who are intentionally inviting of themselves and others, personally and professionally (Purkey & Novak, 1984).

In their study of highly successful business organizations, Collins and Porras (1994) concluded that

> the essence of a visionary company [school, district] comes in the translation of its core ideology and its own unique drive for progress into the very fabric of the organization—into goals, strategies, tactics, policies, processes, cultural practices, management behaviors, building layouts, pay systems, accounting systems, job designs—into everything that the company does. A visionary company [school, district] creates a total environment that envelopes employees [students, teachers, parents, support services, etc.], bombarding them with a set of signals so consistent and mutually reinforcing that it's virtually impossible to misunderstand the company's ideology and ambitions. (pp. 201–202)

From this perspective, an invitational framework has the potential to be more a "theory of everything" than simply a theory of action. The first test of a theory of everything for a school or district is, Does it enhance the learning of all students? Does it conform to our fundamental purpose: student learning? The second test is, Does it fit our core values? Does it communicate to our students, teachers, parents, and other key stakeholders that they are able, valuable, and responsible? When we organize our schools to create separate tracks (streams, bands), are we promoting the learning of *all* students? What messages are we communicating to the students and teachers in each of the tracks? When we decide to cut the budget for the arts and increase the science budget, what are we actually saying about the purposes of education and about those students who may thrive in the arts but struggle in science? This invitational theory of everything obliges us as educators to reflect on the messages behind our actions and, more important, to invite all students to learn in a climate of trust, respect, optimism, and intentionality.

——————— ✿ ———————

There are two aspects of leadership that should not change: one's commitment to "deep" learning for all students, and the life-affirming values that inspire learning, teaching, and caring.

There are two aspects of leadership that should not change: one's commitment to "deep" learning for all students, and the life-affirming values that inspire learning, teaching, and caring. To become a leader of learning, however, existing leaders and prospective leaders alike need to enhance the qualities they were born with, and to learn more about leadership for learning. It is to these two topics I now turn.

QUALITIES

While there is no magic template for educational leadership, most of us have the capacity to assume an important direct or indirect leadership role in a school or district through the appropriateness of our invitations to others. To do so, we must use all of the intellectual qualities that each of us possesses. While few of us are born leaders, each of us is equipped from birth with a set of intellectual qualities or "tools" that are vital to leadership. When we walk out the door in the morning, we all carry an intellectual tool kit that serves us throughout life (Saul, 2001). John Ralston Saul, Canada's foremost contemporary philosopher, has identified six interrelated qualities or tools that we all possess individually and collectively: reason, ethics, common sense, imagination, intuition, and memory. Some of these so-called tools are well developed, while others are underused. How we develop and use these tools determines our leadership potential. Successful leaders develop and employ all of these qualities in a balanced way to meet the challenges of contemporary leadership.

THE TOOL KIT

What makes us unique as humans is our ability to consider and to make choices. Between stimulus and response, humans can make choices; we have free will. We have the ability to shape events in our lives as opposed to being shaped by circumstances. The key word is *ability*. We may or may not use it, or circumstances may be so overwhelming that our ability is unequal to the challenge; however, "to embrace this ability we need tools—qualities—which allow us to free ourselves from our own psychodrama at least long enough to consider real questions in real contexts" (Saul, 2001, p. 3).

In his book *On Equilibrium,* Saul (2001) argues that we can learn to use each of our qualities simultaneously and effortlessly: "We can normalize the use of them so that much of the time we hardly need to stop in order to consider." Through these qualities we "can shape and direct our talents and characteristics—both ours and society's" (p. 5). Each of these qualities, he explains, "takes its meaning from the other—from the tension in which they exist with each other" (p. 13). Isolated, they can become distorted. Ethics can become fanaticism, reason can become irrationality, imagination can become fantasy, memory can become nostalgia, intuition can become superstition and bigotry, and common sense can become nonsense. Together and in equilibrium, they are powerful; isolated, they become distorted into ideology. "After all, ideology is the easiest mechanism for leading the way. Why? Because it makes the large world small. And seemingly certain" (p. 16).

Reason. For the most part, both management programs and the educational literature perseverate on the primacy of reason over other ways of knowing—not "reason" in the sense of "thought and argument," but rather "instrumental reason" that is concerned with form, function, and measurement. By aligning what teachers teach, how they teach it, and how we know they have taught it, technocrats have elevated reason and rationality to a moral principle when it is merely a "disinterested administrative method" (Saul, 1993). The search for "best practice" and the cult of evidence-based decision making that reduces people to numbers and ignores the nonrational aspects of education reflect an ideological rather than a pragmatic stance. Giuliani (2002) contends that "Important, complicated decisions require both statistical analysis and intuition. Statistics can provide the necessary data, but unless you apply your own intuition, gathered from your own experience, you are just a computer spitting out formulas" (p. 154). Reason, as the all-inclusive quality, is pure ideology.

For example, fascist states were built on instrumental reason. Albert Speer, Hitler's henchman responsible for munitions and armament, was the perfect rational technocrat who valued technical systems over social and human systems. As a former architect, he very rationally employed thousands of enslaved Jews, Russians, and other Nazi captives in his armament plants. He was very efficient and very effective in his job. From his ideological perspective, his actions were logical, reasonable, and rational—but quite unethical, indeed reprehensible, by any ethical standards of morality. As Saul comments, "Logic is the art of going wrong with confidence" (p. 124).

This addiction to instrumental reason and rationality has created an educational environment of structures, measurements, targets, and compliance. The search for "best" practice implies that there is one best way to do something. As Collins and Porras (1994) indicate,

> The real question to ask is not "Is this practice good?" but "Is this practice *appropriate* for us—does it fit with our ideology and ambitions?" What makes instrumental reason (utilitarian, instrumental logic) so profoundly irrational is its devotion to mechanistic solutions conceived in a limited time and space, as if the matter at hand were free standing. Instrumental reason exists only because we believe it to be a form of thought, when all we are dealing with is narrow logic built from within. (p. 215, emphasis in original)

Reason unlimited by other qualities will become irrational simply because everything is related to everything else. Our central protection against irrationality, therefore, is the tension between reason and our other qualities. While problem-solving and data-analysis strategies should play an important part in any leadership development program, they need to be presented within a context of the other intellectual qualities.

Ethics. Reason unbalanced by ethics has produced holocausts, arms races, and genocide. Ethics answers the question, How should I live, given the context of the larger good? "The larger good assumes the existence of the *other,* of the family, of the community, of the public good" (Saul, 2001, p. 68, emphasis in original). Archbishop Desmond Tutu expressed this concept well: "I am because you are" (quoted in Coughlan, 2006). This is a stark contrast to the Enlightenment-era credo of Descartes: "I think, therefore I am." Adam Smith (1759/1984) said, "The wise and virtuous man is at all times willing that his own private interest should be sacrificed to the public interest" (p. 235). Ethics in general refers to well-based standards of right and wrong that impose reasonable obligations such as refraining from murder, stealing, and assault and promote such virtues as honesty, compassion, and loyalty. Ethics also applies to standards relating to such rights as the right to life and to privacy.

In education, Starratt (1991) suggests that a fully formed ethical consciousness will contain themes of caring, justice, and reflection on our values and behaviors. Schools are moral places designed to promote certain social norms and to discourage others. School leaders often face ethical dilemmas that require them to choose between two "rights." Do I spend the money on the gifted program that would be politically popular, or on programs for our mentally challenged students? Do I encourage the streaming or tracking (banding) of students, which would certainly please the parents of the high achievers and many of the teachers, or construct heterogeneous classes? Do I allow meetings of religious groups in the school and risk community unrest related to some fringe groups, or ban all religious groups? Do I spend the athletic budget on a football team that involves 30 boys and promotes school spirit and community engagement, or distribute the funds in ways that involve all students? The list is endless. Scholars (Begley & Johansson, 2003) tend to agree that leaders' first step must be to reflect on their own values and then strive to understand the values orientation of others.

> *Schools are moral places designed to promote certain social norms and to discourage others. School leaders often face ethical dilemmas that require them to choose between two "rights."*

Unbalanced by the other qualities, however, ethical solutions could easily slip into extremism: "Good intentions are converted into misplaced certainty as to moral rectitude. This certainty convinces the holder of truth that he has the right to harm others" (Saul, 2001, p. 86). Ethics can lead to fanaticism when extreme ethical positions replace normal behavior in normal times and are not balanced by reason (as thought and argument) and common sense. Religious cults and the Taliban in Afghanistan are but two examples.

Common sense. Common sense is shared knowledge that carries us above self-interest. "Shared knowledge by its very nature is a consideration of the whole. It is essentially inclusive and human" (Saul, 2001, p. 23), and provides a shortcut that allows us to make decisions very quickly. If we depended on pure reason and logic for every decision we make, we would accomplish very little. Common sense, however, knows how to draw conclusions even in the face of incomplete or unreliable information. . . . Common sense knows how to deal with a problem that is so complex it cannot even be specified. Common sense knows how to revise beliefs based on facts that all of a sudden are proved false. Logic was not built for any of these scenarios. (Saul, 2001, p. 23)

Saul (2001) argues that there are two forms of common sense— shared knowledge within society (e.g., education is important) versus superstitions or truths (e.g., private is always superior to public)—that are declared to be visible, evident, and inevitable. These two versions of common sense are continually at war and "so long as we accept the idea of self-evident and therefore inevitable truth—for example, that we are driven by self-interest or technology leads society—our passivity will prepare us for ideological manipulation" (p. 23).

Common sense is the easiest of the qualities to deform into nonsense. It can create a pretense of simplicity and truth that can easily be presented as self-evident, unchallengeable truth. For example, if students are attending school, they have a much better chance of learning the state's curriculum; this is common sense. Since the exclusion from school of some students makes life easier for teachers and principals, some would argue that exclusion is in everyone's best interest. This line of reasoning is an example of "conventional wisdom," or at least unexamined practice that has become false common sense designed to ensure the passivity of others. Similarly, such practices as tracking, age-grade organizations, subject-based curriculum, standardized tests—to name a few examples of the "grammar of schooling" (Tyack & Tobin, 1994)— have remained largely unchallenged and unchanged for years and have become part of what some might consider the commonsense way to organize education.

Imagination. Rolf Jensen of the Copenhagen Institute for Future Studies has suggested,

We are in the twilight of a society based on data. As information and intelligence become the domain of computers, society will place new value on the one human ability that can't be automated: emotion. Imagination, myth, ritual—the language of emotion— will affect everything from our purchasing decisions to how well we work with others. . . . Companies will thrive on the basis of their stories and myths. Companies will need to understand that their products are less important than their stories. (quoted in Peters, 2003, p. 163)

If this is true in the world of business, then it seems to follow that in an age of creativity, imagination is the one quality that educators need to loose the bonds of conformity, control, and compliance. Leaders of learning must not only release their own abilities to imagine, but also create rich, stimulating contexts in which their colleagues can develop their imaginations to create and innovate. Leaders do not necessarily have to generate imaginative solutions to the complex problems that our schools face, but they must be able to recognize and act on creative ideas that emerge from others. Imagination is the quality that allows us to picture a "realistic" future because it most naturally draws all our qualities together. It protects us from premature conclusions: "Just when we think we understand, it leaps ahead again into more uncertainty. And so imagination is naturally inclusive and inconclusive" (Saul, 2001, p. 116). Saul goes on to say, "Imagination is our primary force for progress because it is driven by ideas—incomplete, aggressive, inconclusive ideas." He contends that policies can only survive if they continue to be led by ideas—by the imagination, in other words. "The moment the direction slips into managerial logic, they begin to fall apart, because they are no longer linked directly to the reality and the collective unconscious of society" (p. 118). As he explains,

> *Leaders of learning must not only release their own abilities to imagine, but also create rich, stimulating contexts in which their colleagues can develop their imaginations to create and innovate.*

Those who believe in the dominance of understanding and methodology seem to miss the obvious. The tools they consider marginal—those of the arts—are in fact the tools of story telling and reimagining ourselves, which all humans use. And why do we use them? In order to convince ourselves that we exist as humans and as individuals in a society. (p. 126)

Imagination unlocks our creativity, but it also requires us to develop our inner resources. Imagination and creativity involve not only a passionate interest but a self-confidence too. A person needs a healthy self-respect to pursue novel ideas, and to make mistakes despite criticism from others. Self-doubt there may be, but it cannot always win the day. Breaking generally accepted rules, or even stretching them, takes confidence. Continuing to do so in the face of skepticism and scorn, takes even more. (Boden, 2003, p. 255)

At the same time, leaders will have to be mindful that imagination without the context of the other qualities can lead to fantasy.

Intuition. Wayne Gretzky is generally considered to be the finest ice hockey player in the history of the game. Asked to explain his excellence, he replied, "You must skate to where the puck is going to be, not where it is." His intuition was the product of his experience, his imagination, and his obvious talent. Like other great athletes in "flow," he could slow the play down in his mind and see the entire ice surface and the location of the other players. In a similar vein, Jonas Salk, renowned inventor of the polio vaccine, suggested that intuition is when the intuitive mind tells the logical mind where to go next.

By talking to and watching people in such high-stress, high-risk jobs as firefighting, nursing, and emergency medicine, Klein (2003) discovered that these people did not ask "What do I do?" when confronted by an emergency; instead they intuitively asked, "What is happening here?" By reading the cues and patterns they gleaned from the environment, they moved to action. This is quite the opposite of rational problem solving, in which decision makers develop a range of alternatives and, based on the evidence, choose the best solution. In a crisis this would be folly. For example, once firefighters decide on a course of action, they quickly imagine the results of that action and, assuming that it seems appropriate, take action; if the consequences appear to be too risky, they move to a second option. All of this is done in an instant. The key ingredient that enables these crisis workers to make quality split-second decisions appears to be the extent of their experience. This suggests that intuition is not something mystical that only a few people possess, but rather something that we all possess and with training and experience can develop over time.

As Saul (2001) explains, "The offensive force is the swirling uncertainty of our imagination. Intuition is our reaction to the movement" (p. 163). It is the basis of action that does not have the luxury of slow consideration. Intuition unbalanced by the other qualities, however, has the potential to lead to superstition, bigotry, and crisis management as leaders try to turn uncertainty into certainty—for example, African Americans can't play quarterback, women are too emotional to be principals of secondary schools, and so on. The list is long. "Uncertainty is taken for normal, and the ability to embrace it as a sign of human consciousness as intelligence not fear" (p. 219).

Memory. The final quality, memory, gives us the ability to shape our thinking and our actions in a balanced way. From it we grasp our context, our thoughts, our questions, our actions, and our lives. Memory is the platform from which we initiate thought. Without memory there is a vacuum. Propaganda thrives in a vacuum, as does ideology. "Functioning individuals and functioning societies require the context of memory in order to shape their thinking and their actions" (Saul, 2001, p. 219). An extreme dependence on memory, however, freezes our thoughts and actions in the past and distorts our other qualities. As Saul explains, "A rigid memory pretends to guarantee the future by freezing that of the past" (p. 219). As a result, habit can become a "labor-saving device" (Tyack & Tobin, 1994) and a significant obstacle to change and improvement.

"Memory is part of a seamless web with the future, there to help us remember exactly what our civilization is constructed upon, and therefore, in what ways our civilization is shaped, in order to serve our needs and our interests" (Saul, 1993, p. 136). In some ways, memory is the enemy of the technocrat, who tends to operate as though each new day is just another day and is unconnected to yesterday. How else can we explain society's inability to learn from its mistakes? An understanding of how the school came to be the way it is provides an important contextual basis for understanding the directions it might need to take and some of the impediments that stand in the way of change. Experience is important. Just because a person is experienced, or older, does not necessarily mean that he or she suffers from "hardening of the categories." Leadership develops in large measure from experience—often learning from mistakes that have been made. Learning is a product of our ability to develop these qualities and to focus on what

— ✂ —

Leadership develops in large measure from experience—often learning from mistakes that have been made.

is important in order to achieve in a particular endeavor, such as becoming a leader of learning.

LEARNINGS

Like Jane, Allan, Elena, Charmaine, and other leaders of learning, we can identify and master a set of crucial "learnings" that go across time and space and are at the heart of leadership that promotes students' learning. Taken together, they provide a conceptual framework for the identification, recruitment, training, selection, and ongoing professional development of school leaders. My colleagues Louise Stoll, Lorna Earl, and I have argued that

> Leadership for learning is not a destination with fixed coordinates on a compass, but a journey with plenty of detours and even some dead ends. Effective educational leaders are continuously open to new learning because the journey keeps changing. Their maps are complex and can be confusing. What leaders require for this journey is a set of interrelated "learnings" looking at school leadership in a holistic rather than reductionist way. These "learnings" can be deepened, elaborated, nurtured, abandoned, and connected and related to other "learnings" as the journey progresses. (Stoll, Fink, & Earl, 2003, p. 103)

We have suggested seven sets of "learnings" for leaders of learning that we think go across time and space and apply to all educational leaders. These learnings are

- Contextual knowledge;
- Political acumen;
- Emotional understanding;
- Understanding learning;
- Critical thinking;
- Making connections; and
- Futures thinking.

"Learnings" for Leaders of Learning

To prepare leaders for their future as leaders of learning we need to identify, recruit, prepare, select, induct, appraise, and support leaders around a set of "leaders' learnings" that are not bounded by time and space or collected in huge lists of so-called best practices. These learnings are sufficiently flexible to apply regardless of context or career stage of leaders. Since this topic is dealt with in some detail elsewhere (Fink, 2005; Stoll, Fink, & Earl, 2003), I will address it only briefly here.

Contextual knowledge. Successful leaders make connections by developing a firm knowledge and understanding of their contexts. Context relates to the particular situation, background, or environment in which something is happening. Internal context includes the students, subjects, departments, and the school itself; external context encompasses, among other influences, the district or local education authority of which the school is a part, the school's parents and neighboring community, the relevant employee unions, and any appropriate government(s). The research evidence is fairly clear: schools can only be understood in their context (Hallinger & Murphy, 1986; Teddlie & Stringfield, 1993).

Political acumen. Political acumen is a key "learning" for leaders. At micro levels, schools are filled with groups and individuals with different interests and varying degrees of power that occasionally lead to conflict. Leaders use such political methods as negotiation and coalition building to move schools toward agreed-upon goals. School leaders must also represent the interests of their school with their governing bodies, communities, and government agencies. Politics is about power and influence; to ignore political issues or feel that political activity is unworthy of a leader is to leave the school, its staff, students, and parents vulnerable to competing social forces.

Emotional understanding. Leaders of learning learn to read the emotional responses of those around them and to create emotional bonds with and among those with whom they interact. Hargreaves (1998) explains that the emotions of educational change most commonly addressed are ones that help to defuse so-called resistance to change—trust, support, involvement, commitment to teamwork, and a willingness to experiment. Leaders with emotional understanding do, however, lead their colleagues into uncharted territory on the change journey through the impassioned and critical engagement or critique of ideas, purposes, and practices (Hargreaves, 1998).

Understanding learning. Leaders need to have a deep, current, and critical understanding of the learning process in order to promote learning and to support others' learning. Not only do they need to have insight into "deep" learning for students; they must also have a deep understanding of how adults learn if they are to support teachers' learning and to mobilize the school's human and material resources to this purpose.

Critical thinking. What tends to differentiate effective and ineffective leaders is the quality of their judgments—that is, whether their decisions work for students in the long term. Knowing and remembering to ask the right questions depends on both wisdom and judgment (Secretan, 1996). A significant part of a formal leader's job is to act as a gatekeeper; to ask the right questions; and to know what initiatives to support, what to oppose, and what to subvert. This question-asking facility is a necessary "learning" to enable leaders to help develop a school's capacity to deal with change.

Making connections. It is also a leader's role to see the entire organization and to help stakeholders come to view the school in a holistic way. Leaders provide coherence and make connections so that others can see the interrelationships and interconnections of the many things happening in a school. The development of a schoolwide perspective is an important "learning" to promote positive change.

> *A leader's awareness and understanding of forces influencing the life of a school are crucial to shaping a school community's shared sense of vision in productive and inspiring ways.*

Futures thinking. Successful leaders must learn how to connect the past, the present, and the future. A leader's awareness and understanding of forces influencing the life of a school are crucial to shaping a school community's shared sense of vision in productive and inspiring ways. Leaders are also aware of the shifting currents of local political, social, and economic forces; they help staff to understand the connections between and among global, national, and local forces. Anticipating the future enables leaders to help colleagues act strategically rather than randomly as they journey into the future (Davies & Ellison, 1999).

Elsewhere, Andy Hargreaves and I have described the following seven principles of sustainable leadership:

- Leadership that sustains learning for all students, and that nourishes their development
- Leadership that lasts, that endures over time, that stretches across individuals and that leaves a lasting legacy of deep and enduring learning for students

- Leadership that does not damage the surrounding environment, that does not drain the leadership resources of other schools to support initiatives in one or two lighthouse or showplace schools
- Leadership that can be supported by available or achievable resources—human as well as financial
- Leadership that is a shared responsibility—sustainable leadership that involves everyone and does not rest on the shoulders of the few
- Leadership that is self-sustaining, sustaining selves that have the emotional resources and system support to avoid burnout and maintain their impact over time
- Leadership that promotes diversity and builds capacity throughout the educational environment—that fosters many versions of excellence, and the means of sharing them through powerful learning communities (Hargreaves & Fink, 2006)

CONCLUSION

Many years ago, Jock Carlisle, a teachers college instructor and a rather cryptic and sardonic Scot, used to tell us that "you need some conclusion to your lesson—other than the bell"; he suggested that we leave students with two or three thought-provoking ideas that would link into the next day's lesson. In memory of Jock, I leave you with these summarizing principles of "leadership for mortals":

- Leaders of learning are ordinary people who through extraordinary commitment, effort, and determination have become extraordinary, and have made the people around them exceptional.
- Educational leadership is more art than science; it is more about character than technique; it is more about inspiration than charisma; it is more about leading students' and teachers' learning than the management of things.
- Leaders must be passionately, creatively, obsessively, and steadfastly committed to enhancing "deep" learning for students—learning for understanding, learning for life, learning for a knowledge society.
- Leadership is about communicating invitational messages to individuals and groups with whom the leader interacts in

order to build and act on a shared and evolving vision of a *learning-centered* school.

- We all have the ability to shape events in our lives as opposed to being shaped by circumstances. To embrace this ability, leaders must enhance and employ all of their qualities—reason, ethics, common sense, imagination, intuition, and memory—in equilibrium.

When adapted to an individual's career trajectories, these five principles help to define a leadership model that, with careful management of succession, will successfully develop and sustain leaders of learning over time and space.

NOTES

1. Based on the book of the same name published by Paul Chapman in the UK and Corwin in the United States.

2. A useful way to examine the career stages of leaders is through the concept of "multiple trajectories," described by Etienne Wenger (1998) in his *Communities of Practice*. I develop this in some detail in *Leadership for Mortals* (2005). Inclusion of the concept of trajectories in this model is to suggest that we have to develop our leadership "learnings" and hone our qualities as we progress through our successive career trajectories.

REFERENCES

Begley, P. T., & Johansson, O. (Eds.). (2003). *The ethical dimensions of school leadership.* Dordrecht, The Netherlands: Kluwer.

Boden, M. (2003). *The creative mind: Myths and mechanisms* (2nd ed.). London: Routledge.

Collins, J. C., & Porras, J. I. (1994). *Built to last.* New York: Harper Business Essentials.

Coughlan, S. (2006, September 28). All you need is ubuntu. *BBC News.* Available at http://news.bbc.co.uk/2/hi/uk_news/magazine/5388182.stm.

Covey, S. (1989). *The 7 habits of highly effective people: Powerful lessons in personal change.* New York: Simon & Schuster.

Csikszentmihalyi, M. (2004). *Good business: Leadership, flow, and the making of meaning.* New York: Penguin Books.

Davies, B., & Ellison, L. (1999). *Strategic development and direction of the school.* London: Routledge.

Fink, D. (2005). *Leadership for mortals: Developing and sustaining leaders of learning.* London: Paul Chapman.

Gardner, H. (1996). *Leading minds: An anatomy of leadership.* New York: Basic Books.

Giuliani, R. (2002). *Leadership.* New York: Miramax Books.

Glasser, W. W. (1997). A new look at school failure and school success. *Phi Delta Kappan, 78*(8), 596–602.

Hallinger, P., & Murphy, J. (1986). The social context of effective schools. *American Journal of Education, 94*(3), 328–355.

Hargreaves, A. (1994). *Changing teachers, changing times.* London: Cassell.

Hargreaves, A. (1998). The emotional politics of teaching and teacher development: With implications for educational leadership. *International Journal for Leadership in Education, 1*(4), 316–336.

Hargreaves, A., & Fink, D. (2006). *Sustainable leadership.* San Francisco: Jossey-Bass.

Klein, G. (2003). *Intuition at work: Why developing your gut instincts will make you better at what you do.* New York: Doubleday.

Kouzes, J. M., & Posner, B. Z. (2003). *Credibility: How leaders gain and lose it, why people demand it.* San Francisco: Jossey-Bass.

Louis, K. S., & Kruse, S. D. (Eds.). (1998). *Professionalism and community: Perspectives on reforming urban schools.* Thousand Oaks, CA: Corwin.

Malloy, K. (1998). *Building a learning community: The story of New York City Community School District #2.* Pittsburgh, PA: Learning Research and Development Center, University of Pittsburgh.

Meier, D. (1995). *The power of their ideas: Lessons for America from a small school in Harlem.* Boston: Beacon Press.

Mintzberg, H. (2004). *Managers not MBAs: A hard look at the soft practice of managing and management development.* San Francisco: Berrett-Koehler.

Newman, F. M., & Associates. (1996). *Authentic achievement: Restructuring schools for intellectual quality.* San Francisco: Jossey-Bass.

Nichols, S., & Berliner, D. (2007). *Collateral damage: How high-stakes testing corrupts America's schools.* Cambridge, MA: Harvard University Press.

Peters, T. (2003). *Re-imagine! Business excellence in a disruptive age.* New York: DK Publishing.

Purkey, W., & Novak, J. (1984). *Inviting school success* (2nd ed.). Belmont, CA: Wadsworth.

Saul, J. R. (1993). *Voltaire's bastards: The dictatorship of reason in the West.* Toronto, Ont.: Penguin Books Canada.

Saul, J. R. (2001). *On equilibrium.* Toronto, Ont., Canada: Penguin/Viking.

Secretan, L. H. (1996). *Reclaiming the higher ground: Creating organizations that inspire the soul.* Toronto, Ont., Canada: Macmillan.

Sergiovanni, T. (2004). Building a community of hope. *Educational Leadership, 61*(8), 33–37.

Smith, A. (1984). *The theory of moral sentiments.* Indianapolis, IN: Liberty Fund. (Original work published 1759)

Starratt, R. (1991). Building an ethical school: A theory of practice in educational leadership. *Educational Administration Quarterly, 27*(2), 185–202.

Stoll, L., & Fink, D. (1996). *Changing our schools: Linking school effectiveness and school improvement.* Buckingham, UK: Open University Press.

Stoll, L., Fink, D., & Earl, L. (2003). *It's about learning and it's about time.* London: Routledge/Falmer.

Stoll, L., & Seashore Louis, K. (2007). *Professional learning communities: Divergence, depth, and dilemmas.* Buckingham, UK: Open University Press.

Teddlie, C., & Stringfield, S. (1993). *Schools make a difference: Lessons learned from a 10-year study of school effects.* New York: Teachers College Press.

Tyack, D., & Tobin, W. (1994). The grammar of schooling: Why has it been so hard to change? *American Educational Research Journal, 31*(3), 453–479.

Wenger, E. (1998). *Communities of practice: Learning, meaning, and identity.* New York: Cambridge University Press.

Williams, P. (2002). *The paradox of power.* New York: Warner/Faith.

CHAPTER FIVE

LIBERATING LEADERSHIP POTENTIAL

Designing for Leadership Growth

LOUISE STOLL AND DAVID JACKSON

I magine . . . a group of schools in a very challenging part of a city in northern England redesigning themselves to make it possible for every child to achieve his or her full potential.

This part of the country has all the disadvantages associated with postindustrial urban situations: poor housing, low employment rates, widespread poverty, low levels of educational achievement, and pervasively low aspirations. The seven schools—one secondary (high school), five primary (elementary), and one special school— have tended to reflect this. Raising standards of achievement has been an uphill battle. Recruitment and retention of staff have been a constant challenge. Not surprisingly, public perceptions of the schools—and even the self-esteem of those who work in the schools—have been low.

A few years ago, these challenged schools decided to work together as a group (at the time there were five primary schools and one secondary school in the group) to form a "Family of Schools." This made sense for three strong reasons:

1. Together, they could offer a distributed provision for children and young people from birth to age 19 across their entire locality, planning as one school on six separate sites. Separately, they could not.

2. Together, they could work to engage and mobilize their entire community to be educationally aspiring. Separately, they could not.

3. Within the various schools, there was enough leadership capacity and sufficient pockets of success to build something exciting—together.

So two of the headteachers (principals) agreed to act as "system redesigners" and "placeshapers" to mobilize leadership around these aspirations. The schools committed themselves to a common endeavor: working together for every child's success and creating the leadership capacity to make that goal happen. They set up an Active Learning Team that included representatives from each school and empowered them to visit advanced sites of practice, both in England and abroad, to gather the best practices. They gave the group support from expert consultants and the time to create and pilot a new learning-skills curriculum (aimed at empowering and liberating learners), to be taught in whole-day units. In addition to serving as change agents, staff developers, implementation coaches, and quality assurers, the group also commissioned an external evaluation.

More than anything else, this group modeled the way in which leadership could be liberated by empowerment and ambitious endeavor.

And, more than anything else, this group modeled the way in which leadership could be liberated by empowerment and ambitious endeavor.

Next came an Aspiring Leaders program across the Family, then a student parliament, and then a Strategic Governance Group created to take responsibility for all areas of provision and work undertaken by the Family. By this point, the Family had formed strategic partnerships with three national agencies, each able to provide its own support for portions of the ambitious plans. One agency designed and delivered the leadership program; one supported approaches to personalized learning; one supported system leadership (defined later as "leadership beyond a single institution") and strategic governance.

As a result of this support, the Family's "system governance" group commissioned five strands of work across the Family: teaching and learning, professional development, safeguarding (a multiservice approach to ensuring that all children receive the support they need), community engagement, and business functions. Each was led by a "leadership partnership" that included one headteacher, members of the Aspiring Leaders group (for whom this was an action-learning task as a part of their leadership course), and a wider team of staff and students.

Recently, one school in the Family advertised for a deputy headteacher (assistant principal) and received a very poor response. In a second advertisement, the Family advertised for a deputy who would be based in one of their schools—and they were overwhelmed with the response. It seems that the idea of working across a local group of schools is very attractive to potential senior leaders.

Family leadership has become endemic and exciting. One teacher said, "I have been working at this school for 30 years and my leadership potential was only discovered 3 years ago!" Another said, "I was spending the last few years of my career putting lights out, and now I feel that I'm lighting fires." One parent leader said, "My father grew up in China where he learned to count by the light of fireflies in the evenings. I left school on this housing estate when I was 14. Now I am helping to grow the system for the children on the estate, and I never thought this could happen to me."

LEADERSHIP POTENTIAL

The above scenario illustrates a response to the leadership challenge being faced by schools in England—and in many other countries. This particular response is one that grows from the inside out, starting with (1) a focus on learning, (2) mobilizing communities, (3) redesigning with a systems perspective, (4) incorporating best learning practices from around the world, and (5) embracing a futures orientation. These five components are the scaffold for this chapter. All are under-pinned by a sixth: the values orientation that must drive 21st-century approaches—the imperative for equity and social justice; the entitle-ment of every child, regardless of social background or cultural roots, to an education that enhances their self-esteem, offers them achieve-ment success, prepares them for life and work, and equips them with enthusiasm for future learning.

Students today are growing up in a dramatically changed, rapidly changing, and complex world, which presents significant challenges for leaders in education. Difficulties with the recruitment of princi-pals in many systems and countries (Pont, Nusche, & Moorman, 2008), combined with impending retirements among many princi-pals, mean that planning for succession is a critical task—and it isn't just succession into the same role. New models of leadership may well be required in order to fashion a new system. New ways of devel-oping leadership interest and potential among a wider group of poten-tial aspirants for a wider set of leadership possibilities are necessary. The challenges of change are also too great for any one leader to manage alone (Ancona, 2005). Indeed, we would argue, they are too great for any one school, district, state, or even nation to tackle alone. Leadership is needed at all of these levels and has to be a shared enterprise, within and between the levels. It has to be a system that connects, not divides. This requires the development of leadership capacity—what we refer to as "lib-erating leadership potential." The potential exists, to be sure; it sim-ply needs to be unleashed, which means nurturing, nourishing, and intentionally designing educational systems that can grow that potential at all levels.

> *Leadership has to be a shared enterprise, within and between the levels. It has to be a system that connects, not divides. This requires the development of leadership capacity—what we refer to as "liberating leadership potential."*

DESIGNING FOR LEADERSHIP GROWTH

The type of approach we believe will best address the needs of young people—our future leaders—is underpinned by the five per-spectives that we mentioned briefly above:

1. *A learning perspective*—an orientation to growth, openness to new ideas, and willingness to "learn, unlearn, and relearn" because "Sustainable and continuous learning is a given of the twenty-first century" (Stoll, Fink, & Earl, 2003, p. xv)

2. *A community perspective*—commitment to the values of mutual growth, reciprocity, and interdependence; a belief that reflective collaborative activity with other educators and the wider community can reap greater benefits than we are now realizing, raising the achievement of all while also closing the achievement gaps

3. *A systems perspective*—thinking about the system as a whole; believing that the interrelationship and interdependence among different levels and parts of the system is critical; a multilevel approach to influence the system and leadership at all levels

4. *An international perspective*—understanding that global forces affect educators worldwide, and that a broader cultural orientation not only brings a wealth of diverse new ideas, but can also help bring one's own situation into sharper perspective

5. *A futures perspective*—attending to the forces that affect the context within which learning occurs; focusing on best practice for now but also encouraging innovative "next practice" for the future (Hannon, 2006)

In the rest of this chapter, we draw on our research and development experiences in England and several other countries, looking at how these perspectives come together in schools, local educational systems, national systems, and international systems that are designed to promote leadership growth.

SCHOOLS THAT LIBERATE LEADERSHIP POTENTIAL

Schools have immense power to develop leadership among their staff and students, though truly realizing this power would mean letting go of historical models of leadership in which seniority and length of service determine upward movement, in which leadership is conflated with role, and in which a heroic principal often heads up the enterprise. It also requires that they rethink the power relationships between adults and young people. Increasing leadership capacity in schools means increasing the capacity of others. Enhancing capacity essentially means building a community with the skills, culture, and internal conditions and permissions that enable it to take charge of and manage change, ensuring that it is productive and that it promotes learning for all. Building leadership capacity is necessary if improvement is to be more than a temporary phenomenon. If sustainability is to be ensured, leadership has to be distributed within the school and embedded within its culture.

Leadership capacity is developed in those schools in which senior leaders pay attention to developing as a team. Developing team leadership has been the focus of a research and development project involving one of us. The project entailed working with senior leadership teams in 11 primary and secondary schools in an English school district and with a leadership team from the district. These teams were learning new ways to demonstrate creative leadership: "an imaginative and thought-through response to opportunities and to challenging issues that inhibit learning at all levels" (Stoll & Temperley, 2009).

Creative leadership is about seeing, thinking, and doing things differently in order to improve the life chances of all students. Creative leaders also provide the conditions and opportunities for others to be creative.

Creative leadership is about seeing, thinking, and doing things differently in order to improve the life chances of all students. Creative leaders also provide the conditions and opportunities for others to be creative. We have spent several days together with external facilitators who challenged the teams with new ideas and futures thinking approaches, encouraging them to push boundaries and taking them out of their comfort zones. They had had time to reflect together on these ideas in relation to their own familiar contexts and to develop new strategies. We also introduced processes intended to help the team members consider and develop their own team's learning community. When asked how the learning of senior leadership teams could be enhanced, a new assistant headteacher in one project school replied,

Time to share and reflect on values and to think strategically about their direction. . . . It's not a tangible thing, but I've learned so much from working with the others in that shared time.

For a headteacher of another school, the same learning experience

enabled me to see where they're [the other team members are] comfortable and where they're not; where they're vulnerable. Because we're all learning and out of our comfort zone, it's given them the opportunity to debate with me in a good way.

It is also critical to think much more broadly about developing leadership capacity. Given space limitations, we shall not discuss individual teacher leadership development in this chapter. Rather, our own work and perspectives on community lead us to focus on the role of professional learning communities (e.g., Stoll & Louis, 2007) in fostering wider leadership development. We are concerned about the number of jurisdictions that now "mandate" professional learning communities as a way of raising test scores. This fundamentally goes against their purpose, which we define as building capacity for everyone's continuous and sustainable learning (Bolam et al., 2005). Of course, all efforts to improve schools must lead to a positive difference in all students' learning and life chances, as the following definition of professional learning communities highlights:

[A]n inclusive group of people, motivated by a shared learning vision, who support and work with each other, finding ways, inside and outside their immediate community, to enquire on their practice and together learn new and better approaches that will enhance all pupils' learning. (Stoll et al., 2006, p. 5)

Commitment to these processes, however, must be generated by professionals themselves. Otherwise, collective responsibility will not develop, and this collective responsibility is an essential quality of all true professional learning communities, and is critical in motivating professional accountability. Being collectively responsible for all students' learning indicates the kinds of distributed leadership in professional learning communities that "do more than exemplify the cliché that everyone is a leader; they create the conditions and encouragement where everyone comes forward to lead with purpose and positive intent" (Hargreaves & Fink, 2007, p. 560). In such communities, teachers and other staff feel a sense of "vertical trust" (Sprenger, 2004) between themselves and a school's senior leaders, which enables them to take the risks required when leading peers in new collaborative learning initiatives. In our experience, these teachers are sometimes relatively new to the school and to their career; they bring fresh perspectives to the school. Principals and other senior leaders need to provide such teachers with opportunities and support, as well as be willing to take a back seat and create a culture where failure and success are treated equally as opportunities for further learning. We have come across many teachers and support staff whose leadership capacity has been developed as they have led colleagues in collaborative inquiry projects, taken the lead in planning and supporting the professional learning of colleagues, led school and community programs, and worked with student leaders—among many examples.

Student leadership is also a great untapped resource in our schools. Per Dalin (1998) from Norway has dedicated his career to leading programs of systemic change in underprivileged environments around the world. One of his key messages is that schools must become laboratories for learning, using the capacity of everyone within them to constantly experiment and inquire into new and better ways of doing things. He has estimated that 90 percent of the intellectual capital and leadership potential of a school is underused—and that 95 percent of that underutilization lies in the student body.

There are six compelling reasons why student leadership strategies make sense:

- *Educational values*—Students are people who matter in schools.
- *Community values*—Whose school is it?
- *Rights*—Students are (or should be) a significant voice in schools.
- *Social responsibilities*—Young people have rights and responsibilities that are now enshrined in international law through the 1990 UN Convention on the Rights of the Child.
- *Legitimacy*—The authenticity of student perspectives about learning and the school community is of paramount importance.
- *Pragmatics*—If students are not allowed to change what *they* do, then we will never transform learning.

Tony Townsend (2004) argues, "Many people tell me that not all learning happens in classrooms, and they are right. But it sure as hell doesn't happen anywhere else but inside the learner. We need to involve and liberate the learner." Reflecting on this, we propose the following as a way of thinking about how we might indeed "liberate the learner." We must create and enable

1. Powerful cognitive and metacognitive approaches—learners who increasingly understand themselves as learners and can verbalize that understanding;

2. Classrooms characterized by their motivational climate, engagement, and learning behaviors;

3. Relationships that support learning practices and cultures; and

4. School communities characterized by collaborative, aspirational, optimistic, and high-challenge cultures.

These four characteristics are self-evidently consistent with cultures that liberate student leadership. They can also be applied to adults in schools; they are consistent with "leaderful schools" (Green, 2002). Such school cultures are all about valuing people and the learning that results when we liberate both the leadership capacities and the multiple voices of all those who share responsibility for learning success within a school: adults and young people.

> *"Leaderful" school cultures are all about valuing people and the learning that results when we liberate both the leadership capacities and the multiple voices of all those who share responsibility for learning success within a school.*

LOCAL SYSTEMS THAT LIBERATE LEADERSHIP POTENTIAL

Might it be possible to create a local system in which the community collectively sees the development of all of its young people as the future of that community's well-being? Imagine the power of such a vision! In such an environment, success for only some (or differential success for all) would not be an option. The "schooling" system

would do the job of building success experiences for all children—
because equity and social justice matter.

In such a school system,

- Schools and other providers would work together for the children and the community;
- All schools would know what other schools know;
- All children's learning needs and dispositions, cultural her-
  itage and affiliations would be recognized, as would the learning they do in various locations in multiple facets of their
  lives;
- Resources would be available to unite around the purpose of
  using the community and family resources to help every child
  feel valued, safe, affirmed, fulfilled, and self-actualized;
- Schools would collaborate rather than compete;
- All community services for children would work together;
- No children would be favored over others;
- There wouldn't be an accreditation system that caused some
  children to feel a failure, or a system that failed to use its leadership potential!

Imagine . . .

Achieving the transition to this vision will require leadership
that sees the big picture: systems thinking, futures perspectives, and
international perspectives. One way of providing the connection,
collective purpose, and alignment to address these local-system concerns is offered by networks, federations, or collaboratives of
schools that engage in orchestrated "networked learning" (defined as
"rigorous and challenging joint work and enquiry" [Earl, Katz,
Elgie, Ben Jaafar, & Foster, 2006]).

These kinds of concerns lay at the heart of what England's
National College for School Leadership (NCSL) committed to study
in the Networked Learning Communities (NLC) program between
2001 and 2006 (Jackson, 2005b; www.ncsl.org.uk/networked-
index.htm). The NLC program set out to show that "networked
learning"—joint work founded upon learning principles, which
enables effective practice to be developed and tested within context
through collaboration between institutions—appears both to offer a
highly effective method of adaptation and integration *and* an environment within which leadership grows (Lieberman, 2006).

The NLC program was a large-scale "development and inquiry" initiative involving 137 networks (1,500 schools). It was the world's largest network-based initiative, specifically designed to provide national policy, system learning, and practice-based evidence about network design and implementation issues, network size and type, facilitation and leadership, formation processes and growth states, brokerage, system support, and incentivization. It was charged with generating evidence about how and under what conditions networks can contribute to raising student achievement (Earl et al., 2006); the leadership practices that prove to hold the greatest potential for school-to-school learning (Lieberman, 2006); and the new relationships emerging between networks as a "unit of engagement" and their local authority (school district) partners (Jackson & Hannon, 2005).

The evidence from the NLC program and others is compelling (Hill, 2008). For example, the achievement of children attending schools in Networked Learning Communities improved more than it did in other schools; there was a direct correlation between the extent of staff involvement in the network and student achievement; and there was a similar direct relationship between the active involvement of school leaders in the networks and student achievement. There were positive outcomes in terms of staff engagement and motivation as well as leadership development. Lieberman's (2006) "tracer study" also tracked leaders from networks into a variety of significant, wider roles in system leadership.

These networks of schools also engage in partnerships with other agencies that have a stake in improving the life chances of children and young people. The Every Child Matters legislation in the UK, introduced in 2004, and the more recent Children's Plan in 2008, are landmark pieces of legislation. Commitment to the success of every child, and of the whole child, within the context of interagency and community support,

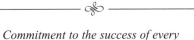

Commitment to the success of every child, and of the whole child, within the context of interagency and community support, offers a radical and inspiring agenda to mobilize leaders in local systems.

offers a radical and inspiring agenda to mobilize leaders in local systems. The idea of public services united around community regeneration, family support strategies, and the success of every child is one that resonates with the moral purposes of the public (state) sector. We simply do not yet know how to do it well and to scale. We do know, though, that solutions will be solved locally and collaboratively, within each particular district or community context. We know also that new models of leadership will be crucial, as will new roles and relationships between tiers of the system (Honig, 2004).

It is possible to imagine, then, such local-system solutions serving their community, committed to social justice and to every child's success. Such an entity (a network, a trust, a federation, a coalition) could be a community resource—an *extended network* rather than an extended school or community school—for all families and members. This entity would be committed to the process of learning together across participating schools and to working in partnership to ensure that aspirations for *all* children are its defining purpose. Its leaders would use all available resources across the area: education professionals and other professionals, parents, technology, finance, and community resources, among others.

This is one vision—and there are others—of how all children could be successful. However, leaders who can make this step—to enact a larger educational vision beyond their schools, to care about all children in the region and to make it happen—are the system leaders and designers we need in the future. They will be educational leaders rather than institutional leaders—and the system will need to grow them from within.

A systems perspective tells us that developing leadership at all levels of the system is absolutely necessary. So, for example, school districts need to develop their own leadership capacity. The creative leadership project we described earlier included a team of middle-level district leaders who didn't know each other well at the start of the project. Together with the school leadership teams, they developed their own team and, in the process, their leadership capacity, including high aspirations and confidence: "[T]he way we developed (in the early stages) as a group, has enhanced self-confidence (self-esteem) and enabled talents/skills to be shared" (Stoll & Temperley, 2008). In a district that promoted coaching in its schools as a form of leadership and teacher learning, the middle-level district leaders' own chosen creative leadership inquiry project was to introduce coaching across the district's advisory team (including the clerical staff). They described this strategy as "high challenge, high risk," adding, "We set high expectations of the project and outcomes (we did not shy away from the difficulties/challenges). We have high confidence as a group to see the project through knowing the CHALLENGE (degree of risk) to *ensure* sustainability" (Stoll & Temperley, 2008, emphasis in original).

This is just one example of inquiry-oriented leadership learning in this district. A key issue here is that school and district leaders worked and inquired together; they learned about leadership together.

STATE AND NATIONAL SYSTEMS THAT LIBERATE LEADERSHIP POTENTIAL

Liberating leadership potential is also the job of governments. School leadership is a powerful national as well as local resource. In England in 2001, the government set up NCSL, cited above, and in 2002 established the Innovation Unit (IU), whose task has been to stimulate and bring discipline to educational innovation, and to raise the profile of practitioner innovation and the forms of leadership that foster it. The Innovation Unit has the job of supporting leaders in their role as system innovators and of harvesting the lessons learned in ways that can facilitate wider learning and also inform emerging policy.

Building on the work of the Networked Learning Communities program and its own early work on collaboration at both the local and the broader system levels (Jackson, 2005a), the Innovation Unit has since 2005 focused its work on developing the concept of *next* practice (as distinct from transferring or disseminating acknowledged "best" or "good" practice) by means of a methodology centered on releasing practitioner (and user) creativity (Hannon, 2006). One strand of this work was the Next Practice in System Leadership program (NPSL).

It is fundamental to this approach that the problems—and solutions—should be those of schools themselves, rather than identified by others. Therefore, schools and local systems were identified that were already pushing at the boundaries of current leadership, governance, and accountability structures. The NPSL program, run in partnership with the NCSL, identified 16 "field trial" sites that comprised various types of collaborations, ranging from whole towns seeking to become "one school," to a formal six-school federation led by a chief executive, to an entire local authority moving toward area-wide "well-being partnerships" of schools and other agencies. (For a full explanation and examples, see www.innovation-unit.co.uk/projects/system-leadership.) The IU supported, challenged, and assisted the 16 sites in developing thinking and practice over a 2-year period up to the end of March 2008. The forms of support employed to stimulate, incubate, and accelerate this work were varied and included the following strategies: consultancy support; tool development and use; strategic change leadership support; peer support; knowledge management techniques, such as support for in-site learning, site-to-site learning strategies and events, community of interest, and online exchange and materials storage; and research and evaluation.

Consistent with our earlier examples, the NPSL program sought to foster different models and advanced practices in locality provision, whereby all services in a defined geographical, local area—groups of 5 to 10 schools, health services, social services, police and youth services—united as one unit with the collective aim of transforming outcomes for young people. It was devoted to encouraging schools to develop models of leadership that will more adequately meet their needs and aspirations—specifically system leadership (defined as "leadership beyond a single institution"). Unless such models can be developed, we argue, it is unlikely that the urgently needed forms of collaboration between and among schools will flourish or be sustained.

The basic details of the NPSL program were the following:

- A total of 16 field trial sites took part—the smallest a small locality, the largest a whole-district transformation program.
- All involved leadership beyond a single institution—most across a locality.
- All had one (or more) of three defining purposes: (1) Every Child Matters implementation and community leadership, (2) federations and "all-through" schools that provide for ages 0–19, and (3) area-wide provision for all students aged 14–19.

The project worked closely with a much wider community of interest that included approximately 1,000 members, comprising other interested sites from which the 16 were chosen, as well as schools and leaders engaged in or wanting to engage in similar innovative work. This community connected with the work through highly developed knowledge management techniques, both face-to-face and virtual (through peer-to-peer online communities). The power of the work lies well beyond the 16 field trials themselves and is likely to extend beyond their local successes, because the Innovation Unit was attempting to act as a "system broker," actively advocating for and facilitating the spread of innovation by connecting learning partnerships to promote a more enduring form of change. In part, this brokerage function has happened directly through the Unit's work; in part, leaders from the sites act as peer leaders with other leaders elsewhere. In addition, the 16 sites were prototypes, advance organizers for system learning, and operational images of practice to be adapted to fit other local contexts.

There are more conventional learnings—insights from the edge of next practices as they transition into new forms of leadership. Among them are the following:

- Governance rather than leadership is the key to sustainability.
- The developmental journey requires transition from one model of system leadership to another.
- These features appear to require brokerage and facilitation at the system level, as described previously.
- New forms of system governance have to define themselves as they explore and develop their new roles.
- There is always enough leadership potential, even in the most complex sites—but it must be liberated, developed, and aligned *in context* (not trained out of context) and toward the collective purpose.
- The appropriate balance of policy incentives and accountabilities can be crucial to success or failure.

There is always enough leadership potential, even in the most complex sites—but it must be liberated, developed, and aligned in context (not trained out of context) and toward the collective purpose.

This short account illustrates a radically new model of state or national support for innovative system leaders. The Innovation Unit advocates for, stimulates, incubates, and makes visible the practices of innovative leaders. It also has the power to arrange for release from any legislative requirements that would act to inhibit leadership aspirations. The Unit, together with young people and communities, are stakeholders in the success of new forms of practice.

A very different approach to the development of systemic leadership that has been unfolding in Austria over the last few years (Leadership Academy, 2007) reinforces the point that approaches to leadership development need to fit the context in which they are embedded. National policy makers, aware of a need for systemic change in the Austrian education system, identified the need to prepare school leaders to lead and sustain systemic change. In 2004, the Minister of Education, Science, and Culture founded the Leadership Academy. Its original intent was to prepare school heads (principals)—who possessed newly acquired autonomy but had little experience in operating outside a hierarchical, bureaucratic structure—with the capacity to act more independently, to take greater initiative, and to manage their schools through changes entailed by a stream of government reforms.

As the benefits to systemic change of involving a wider group of participants became apparent, the Leadership Academy began including district inspectors, staff of teacher training institutes, and executives from the Ministry of Education and provincial education authorities. All of these participants learn together in four forums and work with a learning partner and a collegial coaching team between the forums. The considerable change in relationships, attitudes, and orientation to leadership that appears to be a result of the Leadership Academy for the vast majority of its participants has produced a groundswell at the various levels of the system where people have been involved—schools, districts, regions, teacher training institutes, and parts of the Ministry (Stoll, Moorman, & Rahm, 2007).

While the examples we have cited here come from national systems, the same tenets apply to state systems. The systemwide strategy for building school leadership capacity in the state of Victoria in Australia, for example, has been praised for "the interface between the central leadership, which imbues . . . vision with innovation and momentum, and the framework of leadership development with which schools are inexorably becoming engaged" (Matthews, Moorman, & Nusche, 2007, p. 4). In common with NCSL in England and some other national systems, it offers a range of leadership programs for leaders at different stages of their careers, such as the aspiring leaders in our opening scenario.

INTERNATIONAL SYSTEMS THAT
LIBERATE LEADERSHIP POTENTIAL

Our interconnected world makes it essential that we adopt an international perspective on leadership capacity building. Educators in many countries are dealing with similar learning challenges that are resulting from social, technological, economic, and other global forces that affect all of us. They are also confronting equity challenges that cross national boundaries. We regularly experience the benefits of being part of international learning communities and the enormous value of such communities in enhancing the leadership knowledge and abilities of a wide range of educators. For instance, the International Congress for School Effectiveness and Improvement (ICSEI) serves as a valuable forum where researchers, policy makers, and school and district leaders from many countries come together to share and learn ways to improve students' learning and well-being. The 2008 ICSEI conference in New Zealand attracted people from 32 countries, a considerable number of whom are specifically exploring ways of developing leadership capacity. Jenny Lewis (www.icsei.net), who recently left a school in New South Wales, Australia, to become chief executive officer at the Australian Council for Educational Leaders, feels that

> ICSEI provides me with the opportunity to participate with practitioners, researchers and policy makers from around the world on issues affecting student learning and school improvement. This incredible opportunity to learn from and with such a learned global connected community has ensured my own effectiveness as a school principal of a low socio-economic and disadvantaged school.

In the International Leadership Learning Program, a recently revised program designed by England's National College for School Leadership, networks of headteachers and other senior leaders in schools will have the opportunity to participate in focused and facilitated study visits to other countries; participants will bring back new knowledge both to enhance their own leadership capacity and to share more widely throughout the larger system, serving as an ongoing networked learning community.

The South Gloucestershire Local Authority (school district) in southwest England has been promoting international learning through its own leadership academy, making and hosting visits of groups of leaders and building international professional networks of leaders at various levels who remain connected and continue to learn together. South Gloucestershire leaders who have made focused international visits have implanted many of the ideas they have learned in other leadership academy inquiry activities, thus spreading international perspectives:

> [T]hese international networks have helped school leaders promote their own PLCs [professional learning communities] through a process of continual learning in a no-risk environment, as well as connecting the leaders as a group and between the groups to deepen, extend and enrich the learning community throughout the local authority, thus helping to develop other leaders across schools and the authority. (Stoll, Robertson, Butler-Kisber, Sklar, & Whittingham, 2007, p. 75)

CONCLUSION

Our wide-ranging discussion is both about leadership and about connectedness among the levels of the education system writ large. It is about leadership capacity in different parts of the system. It highlights that we need to think differently about leadership. Already the language of leadership is changing: distributed leadership, learning-centered leadership, lateral leadership, community leadership, leadership capacity, shared leadership, teacher leadership, coleadership—these are far from being merely the latest jargon. Increasingly, they represent a language that is being used to explore new realities.

We opened this chapter with a scenario, one in which new models of practice are being forged to meet local equity and achievement challenges—but which are also national and international challenges. Such examples can act as "advance organizers" for broader learning. When we began working with those schools, we were told, "We need a new leadership paradigm for our work here. The old model is unsustainable; our aspirations are higher than it can deliver."

That, too, is a national and international challenge.

REFERENCES

Ancona, D. (2005). *Leadership in an age of uncertainty.* MIT Leadership Center. Accessed Sept. 2007 from http://sloanleadership.mit.edu/pdf/LeadershipinanAgeofUncertainty-researchbrief.pdf.

Bolam, R., McMahon, A., Stoll, L., Thomas, S., Wallace, M., Hawkey, K., et al. (2005). *Creating and sustaining effective professional learning communities.* DfES Research Report RR637. University of Bristol. Retrieved from www.dfes.giv.uk/research/data/uploadfiles/RB637.pdf.

Dalin, P. (1998). Developing the twenty-first century school: A Challenge to reformers. In A. Hargreaves, A. Lieberman, M. Fullan, & D. Hopkins (Eds.), *International handbook of educational change.* Dordrecht, The Netherlands: Kluwer.

Earl, L., Katz, S., Elgie, S., Ben Jaafar, S., & Foster, L. (2006). *How networked learning communities work.* Final report of the three-year external evaluation of the Networked Learning Communities Programme. Nottingham, UK: National College for School Leadership.

Green, D. (2002). *Leaderful communities: Attending to a "legitimate and unavoidable impatience."* Paper presented to NCSL First Invitational International Conference by the Centre for Evidence-Based Education, New American Schools.

Hannon, V. (2006). *"Next practice" in education: A disciplined approach to innovation.* London: The Innovation Unit.

Hargreaves, A., & Fink, D. (2007). Redistributed leadership for sustainable learning communities. *Journal of School Leadership, 16*(5), 550–565.

Hill, R. (2008). *Achieving more together: Adding value through partnership.* Leicester, UK: Association of School and College Leaders (in association with the Esmee Fairbairn Foundation, and Research Machines).

Honig, M. I. (2004). Where's the "up" in bottom-up reform? *Educational Policy, 18*(4), 527–561.

Jackson, D. (2005a). *Local authority-wide support for school networks: Adaptive change practices at a system level.* Paper presented to the annual meeting of the American Educational Research Association, Montreal, Quebec, Canada.

Jackson, D. (2005b). Networked learning in the public sector: The case of NCSL. In T. Paton, G. Peters, J. Storey, & S. Taylor (Eds.), *Handbook of corporate university development: Managing strategic learning initiatives in public and private domains.* Aldershot, UK: Gower Publishing.

Jackson, D. (2007). *Networked learning communities: Setting school-to-school collaboration within a system context.* Jolimont, Victoria, NSW: Centre for Strategic Education. (Seminar Series, Paper No. 159)

Jackson, D., & Hannon, V. (2005). *Local authority in a network-based system.* Nottingham, UK: National College for School Leadership.

Leadership Academy. (2007). *Leadership academy: Generation I executive summary.* Vienna: Austrian Federal Ministry for Education, Arts and Culture. Available at http://www.leadershipacademy.at/index.en.php.

Lieberman, A. (2006). *System leadership in action: Where do system leaders come from?* Nottingham, UK: National College for School Leadership.

Matthews, P., Moorman, H., & Nusche, D. (2007). *A system-wide strategy for building school leadership capacity in the state of Victoria,*

Australia: A case study report for the OECD activity Improving School Leadership. Paris: Organisation for Economic Co-operation and Development.

Pont, B., Nusche, D., & Moorman, H. (2008). *Improving school leadership. Volume 1: Policy and practice.* Paris: Organisation for Economic Co-operation and Development.

Sprenger, R. K. (2004). *Trust: The best way to manage.* London: Cyan Communications.

Stoll, L., Fink, D., & Earl, L. (2003). *It's about learning (and it's about time).* London: RoutledgeFalmer.

Stoll, L., & Louis, K. S. (2007). *Professional learning communities: Divergence, depth, and dilemmas.* Maidenhead, UK: Open University Press; New York: McGraw-Hill.

Stoll, L., McMahon, A., Bolam, R., Thomas, S., Wallace, M., Greenwood, A., et al. (2006). *Professional learning communities: Source materials for school leaders and other leaders of professional learning.* London: The Innovation Unit. Available at http://www.innovation-unit.co.uk/ index.php?option=com_content&task=view&id=31&Itemid=70.

Stoll, L., Moorman, H., & Rahm, S. (2007). *School leadership development strategies: The Austrian Leadership Academy: A case study report for the OECD activity Improving School Leadership.* Paris: Organisation for Economic Co-operation and Development.

Stoll, L., Robertson, J., Butler-Kisber, L., Sklar, S., & Whittingham, T. (2007). Beyond borders: Can international networks deepen professional learning community? In L. Stoll & K. S. Louis (Eds.), *Professional learning communities: Divergence, depth, and dilemmas.* Maidenhead, UK: Open University Press; New York: McGraw-Hill.

Stoll, L., & Temperley, J. (2008). *Creative Leadership Learning Project: An enquiry project for senior leadership teams and local authority officers in South Gloucestershire—Final report.* Unpublished report. London: Creating Capacity for Learning.

Stoll, L., & Temperley, J. (2009). Creative leadership: A challenge of our times. *School Leadership and Management, 29*(1), 63–76.

Townsend, T. (2004, January). *The accountability game: From rules and regulations to real improvement.* Keynote presentation at the International Congress for School Effectiveness and Improvement, Rotterdam, The Netherlands.

CHAPTER SIX

AGAINST THE ODDS

Successful Leadership in Challenging Schools

ALMA HARRIS

INTRODUCTION

The consequences of growing up poor affect millions of young people worldwide (Knapp 2001; Rainwater & Smeeding, 2003). Global poverty remains a top-priority social and economic issue, and the educational reform agenda in many countries reflects a renewed interest in addressing the relationship between poverty and underachievement. It is clear that the gap between children from low-income families and their more affluent peers persists (Feinstein, 2000; Teese, 2000); in the majority of cases, this gap actually increases throughout schooling (Borman, D'Agostino, Wong, & Hedges, 1998).

While social disadvantage is not an excuse for poor academic achievement, it certainly is a powerful explanatory factor. As Power et al. (2003) conclude, educational outcomes in deprived areas are worse than those in non-deprived areas, whether they are measured in terms of qualification, attendance, exclusions, or the rates at which young people stay in school. Inner-city areas in particular have low educational outcomes. Power et al. also point to the need to reduce the "compositional effects that appear to result from high concentrations of disadvantaged students."

Many young people live in families that are below the poverty line and, as a result, attend school less often, have fewer educational opportunities, and endure poorer health and significantly lower achievement than their more affluent counterparts (Stoll, Fink, & Earl, 2003). Poverty also affects the nonacademic aspects of schooling, such as student self-esteem, antisocial behavior, attentiveness, and peer relations; all these areas of particular focus in schools in high-poverty communities have an important impact on subsequent life chances in terms of employment and salary level. The educational odds, it seems, are still heavily stacked against children from our poorest communities.

Disadvantage can take many forms. It can be reflected in large family units, single-parent families, crowded or temporary housing, weak family networks, and lack of financial and physical resources, along with low self-esteem and poor social skills. Schools serving poorer families can find themselves trapped in an "iron circle" that begins with the family's impoverished economic conditions and may involve unemployment; cultural, racial, or linguistic factors; immigration; high mobility; family breakups; malnutrition and other health problems; substance abuse; and low expectations that include youngsters' performance at school (Leithwood & Steinbach, 2002). One of the distinguishing features of schools in high-poverty communities is the amalgam of problems that young people face and, by association, the problems that staff in the school must deal with on a daily basis.

Teachers in schools facing challenging circumstances must work much harder simply to get to the starting line—the point at which students feel able and willing to learn.

Teachers in schools facing challenging circumstances must work much harder simply to get to the starting line—the point at which students feel able and willing to learn. Many young people from poorer families enter school with a myriad of emotional and behavioral problems that make it more difficult for routine teaching and learning practices to take place. This is not to suggest that these young people cannot or will not learn; in fact, the evidence shows that many schools in challenging circumstances do succeed *against the odds,* but achievement is more difficult and hard won (Harris, Clarke, James, Harris, & Gunraj, 2006).

As schools face increased public and political demands for improved performance, schools in high-poverty communities find it difficult to meet these expectations. Although some schools in difficult circumstances have been successful in raising achievement (Reynolds, Hopkins, Potter, & Chapman, 2001), a significant number are still not making the progress expected of them. Many of the major external intervention programs and current policies have been unable to reverse the educational fortunes of schools serving disadvantaged communities. Recent evidence shows that while some schools in disadvantaged contexts are able to "raise their game," others simply are not able to do so because of powerful socioeconomic forces that persist and ultimately prevail (Harris et al., 2006).

Although some progress has been achieved among schools in high-poverty communities, the size of the gap in performance and the comparatively slow rates of improvement in high-poverty schools present a less than comforting picture (Gray, 2004). It seems that levels of disadvantage still account, in part, for poor attainment and that this relationship is stubbornly resistant to policy intervention. This conclusion is reinforced by a substantial international body of research into the nexus between poverty and education, which demonstrates that, while the attainment levels of poor children have increased over time, the gap between the majority of children from low-income families and their more affluent peers persists throughout schooling (Power et al., 2003; Teese, 2000). It is clear that many schools in disadvantaged areas perform below national norms and that these patterns of performance are well established and continue. In summary, the more socially disadvantaged the community served by the school, the more likely it is that the school will underperform (Rainwater & Smeeding, 2003).

Research also shows the cumulative effect of attending less-effective schools. As Gray (2004) points out, part of being disadvantaged seems to be about having the misfortune to end up attending "poorer" institutions more than chance would predict (p. 306). It remains the case that certain groups of pupils consistently fail to reach their potential, while other groups of pupils consistently succeed, and that children from low-income families do not, on average, overcome the hurdle of lower initial attainment (Power et al., 2003). Poverty therefore remains a powerful indicator of subsequent educational achievement (Gray, 2004, p. 1).

Is Improvement Possible?

Both policy makers and practitioners tend to believe strongly that schools can overcome social disadvantage and can make a difference in the life chances of the most disadvantaged students. This belief is well founded; the literature substantiates the fact that effective schools in disadvantaged communities contribute more to academic performance than effective schools in more affluent areas (Hopkins, 2001; Maden, 2001). They provide the social and emotional support structures often lacking in the home, along with the press for academic achievement. But not all schools in challenging circumstances are effective, and not all schools add such value. So what makes the difference between an effective school in challenging circumstances and a less-effective school?

Clearly the answer to this question is complex and context specific, but one common denominator of all high-performing schools is effective leadership. The fields of both school effectiveness and school improvement have identified strong leadership as one of the most significant correlates of effective and improving schools (Bishop, 1999; Fullan, 2006;

One common denominator of all high-performing schools is effective leadership.

Mortimore, 1993; Townsend, 2007). The research literature consistently emphasizes the powerful relationship between leadership and school improvement, highlighting that principals make a significant difference in school performance (Hopkins, 2001; Van Velzen, Miles, Elholm, Hameyer, & Robin, 1985; West, Jackson, Harris, & Hopkins, 2000). It highlights that strong, successful school leadership can reduce the depressing effects of some of the antecedent conditions of poverty quite dramatically (Leithwood & Steinbach, 2002; Mulford et al., 2007).

Research also shows that while all successful principals tend to exhibit similar leadership practices, these practices need to be deployed in more contextually sensitive and appropriate ways in schools that face challenging circumstances (Day, Sammons, Leithwood, Harris, & Hopkins, 2009). Findings show that effective principals in such schools have to be more responsive to their social and cultural contexts in order to secure lasting improvement (Harris et al., 2006).

Many of the principals who work in schools in high-poverty communities often come from similar socioeconomic backgrounds themselves. Many have deliberately chosen to work in such schools; they display a strong commitment to making a difference in the life chances of the young people with whom they work:

> They have a strong moral purpose but often wrestle with idealism/ pessimism about how much this is possible in practice. Very often they spend long hours at work to the detriment of their health and family life. (Blackmore, 1999, p. 15)

> Principals who work in this context are often prepared to buck the system when necessary, and are willing to resist external interference where they feel it is detrimental to students and staff. (Harris, Muijs, Chapman, Stoll, & Russ, 2003, p. 23)

Successful principals of schools in high-poverty communities also tend to invest more heavily in relationship building to build trust with the community.

> They find resources [time and money] to allow teachers to take up the vital work of professional knowledge production. They work to build up a staff of like-minded teachers and they often develop strong out-of-school friendships with them. The work of leading/managing in difficult schools relies heavily on trust and reciprocity. (Thomson & Harris, 2004, p. 3)

However, as Gray (2001) notes, "We don't really know how much more difficult it is for schools serving disadvantaged communities to improve because much of the improvement research has ignored this dimension—that it is more difficult, however, seems unquestionable" (p. 33). Relatively few studies have focused exclusively on leadership practices within improving schools facing challenging circumstances (SFCC). The reason for this lack of attention lies predominantly in the inherent sensitivity and complexity of performing research in schools in vulnerable and often volatile contexts. Schools that face multiple forms of disadvantage are least likely to be receptive to external scrutiny because they are most often the schools exposed to negative media attention and critical appraisal by policy makers. The studies we do have of high-performing schools in high-poverty communities point to the influence and central importance of certain leadership practices.

This chapter outlines the findings from two studies of successful leadership in secondary and primary (elementary) schools in England. It outlines the key features of successful leadership practices in SFCC and highlights some of the strategies for improvement adopted by principals within each school. It concludes by considering the long-term prognosis for improving schools that face difficult or challenging circumstances.

SUCCESSFUL LEADERSHIP IN SCHOOLS IN CHALLENGING CIRCUMSTANCES

In 2002, a research study in England explored the leadership practices of successful principals in schools facing challenging circumstances (Harris & Chapman, 2002). In 2006, a study commissioned by the Department for Children, Schools and Families (DCSF), in conjunction with the National College of School Leadership (NCSL), focused on the critical relationship between school leadership and improved pupil learning outcomes (Leithwood, Day, Sammons, Harris, & Hopkins, 2007). Both studies explored the leadership approaches of successful principals and collected data about leadership in schools in challenging circumstances.

It was clear from both data sets that *context* played an important part in the way leadership was understood and deployed in the subject schools. The evidence collected within the studies suggests that principals adopt leadership approaches that match the particular stage of a school's development and that are most appropriate to the school's context. All the principals tended to adopt leadership approaches that empowered others to lead. They also enabled teachers to engage in real leadership tasks that contributed directly to improvements in teaching and learning. This "distributed" form of leadership is similar in many ways to transformational leadership, both in its orientation and aspiration (Harris et al., 2006; Leithwood & Jantzi, 2000).

All the principals tended to adopt leadership approaches that empowered others to lead. They also enabled teachers to engage in real leadership tasks that contributed directly to improvements in teaching and learning.

The studies found that while the principals' responses to problems varied, depending on the circumstance or situation, their value position remained consistently one of involving students, staff, and parents in seeking solutions to the problems facing the school. This value position extended to other agencies outside the school; the principals were aware that many of the difficulties they encountered with young people originated in circumstances external to the school. While the principals acknowledged that they had all adopted autocratic leadership approaches at critical times, when firm direction was needed, they also agreed that this leadership approach was least likely to contribute to sustained school improvement.

The findings suggest that leadership in schools facing challenging circumstances is primarily concerned with creating a culture of high expectations that allows young people to feel valued and where high-quality teaching and learning is of paramount importance. This form of leadership is people-centered and primarily concerned with generating improvement capacity within the organization by encouraging others to lead.

VISION AND VALUES

Of central importance to leaders in SFCC was the cooperation and alignment of others with their own set of values and vision. The principals communicated their personal vision and belief systems by direction, words, and deeds. All of the principals had deliberately chosen to work in SFCC. Their vision and values emanated from a core belief in the ability of all children to learn and in the school's potential to offset the effects of disadvantage on student performance.

The principals regularly communicated this vision to staff and parents. The data showed that through a variety of symbolic gestures and actions, they were successful at aligning staff, parents, and students with their particular view of what the school stood for and how it should operate. These principals displayed a great optimism about learning, and all of them subscribed to the view that within their school there was huge potential for student growth and development. They respected others and treated each person as an individual. They trusted others and required trust *from* others. They recognized the need to be actively supportive, caring, and encouraging, as well as challenging and confrontational when necessary.

> I lead through making my values explicit to others and motivating them to believe in the same vision of what the school could be. (Principal)

> The principal's values are clear and made explicit in his actions. He leads through his values, and these are pretty well shared within the school. (Teacher)

The vision and practices of these principals were organized around a number of core personal values that included the modeling and promotion of respect for individuals, fairness and equality, caring for the well-being and whole development of students and staff, integrity, and honesty. It was clear from everything said by the principals that their leadership values and visions were primarily moral (i.e., dedicated to the welfare of staff and students, with the latter at the center) rather than primarily instrumental (for economic reasons) or non-educative (for custodial reasons). Their values and vision shaped their relationships with staff and students and were also informed by these relationships.

The principals displayed people-centered leadership in their day-to-day dealings with individuals. Their interaction with others was based on respect and trust, and they shared a commitment to developing the potential of all staff and all students.

> The principal's main aim is to allow others to flourish and grow—whether staff or students, it doesn't matter. The aim is to develop others and to generate self-belief and self-esteem in those that currently lack it. (Teacher)

> People are your greatest asset, and I firmly believe therefore that the staff and the students in this school are my best resource for change. (Principal)

These principals' ability to invite others to share and develop their own vision was frequently commented on by both staff and students. Along with these qualities, however, were examples of principals being firm (in relation to values, expectations, and standards) and, on occasion, making very tough decisions, e.g., initiating competency proceedings against teachers who consistently under-performed. These principals did not gently cajole staff and students toward success, but recognized that balancing pressure and support while building positive relationships was of prime importance. In many respects, *the way the principals interacted with others was the common denominator of their success.* The human qualities they possessed enabled them to lead others effectively and to establish confidence in others that their vision was worth sharing.

DISTRIBUTING LEADERSHIP

The principals adopted highly creative approaches to tackling the complex demands of implementing multiple changes. The decision to work with and through teams as well as individuals was a common response to the management of change. The principals used a number of strategies for bringing out the best in their staff. In addition to formal development opportunities, these strategies included the power of praise, involving others in decision making, and giving professional autonomy. Although the principals tended to concentrate on their teaching staff, they used similar approaches when dealing with local administrators, parents,

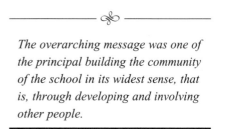

The overarching message was one of the principal building the community of the school in its widest sense, that is, through developing and involving other people.

and (to some extent) students. All the principals invested in others in order to lead the school. From the perspectives of these others, the overarching message was one of the principal building the community of the school in its widest sense, that is, through developing and involving other people.

> When I first came to the school, the principal and senior management team were considered to be the leaders; everyone else opted out. With the formulation of teams with clear targets, I've been able to distribute leadership and to energise teachers to take responsibility for change and development. (Principal)

> The principal has given real leadership responsibilities to others. It's not a case of just delegating tasks. (Teacher)

The middle managers now have greater responsibility and authority for leading. The days of being in charge of stock cupboards are over. (Assistant Principal)

Principals in the studies consistently highlighted the importance of possessing a range of leadership strategies in order to address the diverse sets of issues and problems they faced. They also emphasized the contingent nature of many of the decisions they made and how different leadership strategies would need to be used in different contexts. An important contributing factor in achieving a positive outcome was considered to be how the principal's leadership style matched the situation or circumstance facing the school at different times.

It's a learning curve all the time. I think leadership styles have to match the needs of that school at that particular point in time. (Principal)

The principal displays a range of leadership styles, really; much depends on the situation or circumstance. (Teacher)

I don't think there is one leadership style or approach, is there? Any more than there is a single teaching style. You need breadth and diversity in both. (SMT Teacher)

In particular, the principals emphasized that while they adhered to a broad set of values, they did not feel that their values necessitated a fixed approach to leadership. They felt strongly that they could switch to a leadership style that suited the situation and behave in ways that did not reflect their core beliefs, if necessary.

LEADING LEARNING

For these principals, effective leadership was centrally concerned with building the capacity for improved teaching and learning. The principals were quick to dispel the "cultural deficit" notion prevalent in so many SFCC; they were committed to the belief that *every* child can learn and succeed. They made decisions that motivated both staff and students and placed an emphasis on student achievement and learning. The principals talked about *creating the conditions that would lead to higher student performance,* and they were deeply concerned about the welfare and the educational experiences of minority children.

The principals set high expectations for students, emphasized consistency in teaching practices, and provided and emphasized clear rules about behavior and discipline. Their developmental focus, however, was on improving the quality of teaching and learning. In this sense, they were instructional leaders as the emphasis was on student attainment and achievement.

> The principal has reoriented our attention to the classroom level. We are encouraged to share ideas and to talk about teaching rather than how individuals behave in class. (Teacher)

> The predominant culture in this school was one where teachers discussed issues of teaching and learning very rarely. In fact, everything else but that! The principal has changed that. He has positively encouraged debate and discussion around classroom issues, which has been a welcome change. (SMT Teacher)

The principals created learning opportunities for both students and teachers. They focused their strategic attention on the classroom and engaged staff in dialogue about teaching and learning issues rather than issues of behavior or classroom management. They were able to make clear links between their core values and their vision for improved student achievement and learning.

INVESTING IN STAFF DEVELOPMENT

A central concern for principals was maintaining staff morale and motivation. In a number of the schools, staff morale had been low and individual self-esteem had been eroded by continuing external criticism of the school. Consequently, the principals consistently and vigorously promoted staff development, whether through in-service training, visits to other schools, or peer support schemes. It was noticeable also that such development focused not only on meeting needs that were of direct benefit to the school, but also those of direct benefit to the individual. The development needs of non-teaching staff were also included. The emphasis principals placed on the continuing development of their staff was an endorsement that teachers were the schools' most important asset and that, especially in difficult times, it was important to boost teachers' sense of self-worth by showing them that they were valued.

> Teachers in this school have had their morale eroded and chipped away by successive inspection. It is important to invest in them and their capabilities, to raise morale and to foster "can do" culture. (Principal)

> If you are constantly told you are failing, you believe it. You are a failed teacher. (Teacher)

The emphasis placed on the continuing development of their staff reflected the recognition among principals that the teachers were their most important resource. Consequently, they were highly skilled at using a combination of pressure and support to promote the efforts of teachers, particularly when working with the most difficult students. They encouraged teachers to take risks and rewarded innovative thinking.

The emphasis placed on the continuing development of their staff reflected the recognition among principals that the teachers were their most important resource.

The principals set high standards for teaching and teacher performance. The focus and emphasis on improving teaching and learning were common across all schools in the studies. Time was provided to allow teachers to discuss teaching approaches, and teachers were able to observe each other's teaching. In addition, teaching performance was monitored and individual assessments made. Poor teaching was not ignored or tolerated within the schools. Where it did exist, it was challenged and strategies were arranged for improvement. Where improvement did not occur, the principal took the necessary steps to deal with the problem. In the majority of cases, a combination of structured support, monitoring, and an individual development plan addressed the problem of poor teaching. For these principals, effective leadership was about capacity building and investing in the social capital of the school.

RELATIONSHIPS

The principals were skilled at developing and maintaining relationships. They were considered to be fair and were seen as having a genuine joy and vibrancy when talking to students. They generated a high level of commitment in others through their openness, honesty, and the quality of their interpersonal relationships. The principals engaged in self-criticism and were able to admit to others when they felt they had made a mistake. They placed special emphasis on generating positive relationships with parents and fostering a view of the school as being part of rather than apart from the community.

> It is important that staff and students are involved in the life of the school and relate to each other in a positive way. (Principal)

> The principal has ensured that we work more in teams and work across our subject areas. This has made us build broader relationships and work together. (Teacher)

Principals in the studies emphasized *people rather than systems* and invited others to lead. It was clear that while they possessed a range of leadership strategies to address the diverse sets of issues and problems they faced, at the core of their leadership practice was a belief in empowering others.

> Ultimately, the job of the leader is to give others the confidence and capability to take on new responsibilities. It's really about giving power to others rather than keeping it at the top. (Principal)

> In many respects we have more power than before. We are involved in decision making; we are able to take ideas forward and to challenge new ideas and developments. I guess we are more involved, more part of the decision-making process than before. (Teacher)

> The principal has deliberately devolved leadership to others. I was concerned at first that this would mean we would lose control over the management of the school, but it has generated much more interest from the staff in being involved in decisions. There is less apathy and less resistance to change. (Assistant Principal)

While the principals emphasized the contingent nature of many of the decisions they made and how different leadership strategies would be used in different contexts, the central belief in distributing leadership to teachers remained unaltered. This form of leadership starts not from the basis of power and control but from the ability to act with others and to enable others to act. It places an emphasis on empowering others to lead.

COMMUNITY BUILDING

A distinctive feature of schools that are improving is how well they work as a *professional learning community*. Within the schools in the studies, a climate of collaboration existed and there was a commitment among most staff to work together. It is important to note, however, that this climate was the result of lengthy discussion, development, and dialogue among those working within and outside the school. It was deliberately orchestrated through the provision of opportunities to build social trust. This included providing opportunities for dialogue between staff and parents. The principals emphasized the need to establish an *interconnectedness of home, school, and community*. This included adopting a multiagency approach to problem solving, as well as understanding the wider needs of the community.

The principals were acutely aware of the need to engage with their community. They visited homes, attended community events, communicated regularly with parents about successes, and engendered trust by showing genuine care for young people. They understood the forces within the community that impeded learning, they were aware of the negative forces of the various subcultures, and they listened carefully to parents' views and opinions. The principals tried to create integral relationships with the families in the communities they served. They recognized that family, school, and community relationships directly affected student outcomes—hence the need to connect with the community was of paramount importance to the success of the school.

The principals recognized that family, school, and community relationships directly affected student outcomes—hence the need to connect with the community was of paramount importance to the success of the school.

This school is located on the edge of a large sprawling council estate. There is long-term unemployment, low aspirations, and high levels of crime and drug abuse. The biggest problem we had was getting the community to see us as a resource rather than the enemy. (Deputy Principal)

The principals were also highly responsive to the demands and challenges placed on their school by other external forces. SFCC often receive far more attention and intervention from the district and central government levels than do schools in more affluent settings. Schools in challenging circumstances are often under constant scrutiny and pressure to implement numerous innovations and interventions. The principals saw their role as protecting teachers from unnecessary intrusions or burdens by acting as gatekeepers to external pressures. While there were certainly innovations and new initiatives at each school, these had been carefully selected to ensure that they would enhance the school's development plan and would not simply compete for teachers' classroom time and energy.

The findings from both studies highlight that successful principals in schools facing challenging circumstances display the same repertoire of basic leadership practices. This includes building vision and setting directions, understanding and developing people, redesigning the school's organization, and managing the teaching and learning program. These approaches, however, tend to be mediated by context, with principals in SFCC displaying a broader range of strategies in order to implement and manage change.

WHAT DO WE KNOW?

The research provides a sound basis for understanding leadership practices in schools in challenging circumstances. So what does it tell us? First, it highlights the central importance of an agreed-upon, shared set of values and vision. Establishing a clear vision and communicating a sense of direction for the school are critical tasks for leaders in SFCC.

Second, the evidence shows that successful principals in SFCC tend to distribute certain strategic leadership responsibilities or core developmental work to teams or individuals within the school. While principals in SFCC clearly recognize the need to take responsibility for *all* decisions made, they also acknowledge the importance of empowering teachers who are not necessarily in positions of responsibility or authority to lead important initiatives or developments on behalf of the school.

Third, it is clear that principals in SFCC strongly emphasize pupil achievement and learning, and those conditions that can lead to higher student performance. They set high expectations for students, emphasize consistency in teaching practices, and provide clear rules about behavior and discipline. Their central developmental focus is on improving the quality of teaching and learning. In this sense, they are instructional leaders. In short, successful leaders in schools facing challenging circumstances ensure that improving the quality of teaching and learning is at the center of all development work, and they ensure that all teachers focus on this priority.

Fourth, successful leaders in all schools recognize the importance of staff development as a powerful lever for change and development. In schools in difficulty, staff development is also a very important means of maintaining staff morale and motivation. The emphasis placed on the continuing development of teachers is not only a clear endorsement that teachers are valued within the school, but also a way of recognizing that their professional learning is important. It also secures and maintains positive relationships among staff as it encourages collaboration and sharing of ideas. Finally, successful leaders in schools in difficult contexts are acutely aware of the need to engage their community and to engage parents in supporting learning.

Recent research on successful school principals (Mulford et al., 2007) has provided additional insights into successful leadership in high-performing schools in high-poverty communities. It suggests that these principals

- Spend less time out of their schools;
- Spend more time working with students;
- Place more importance on managing tensions and dilemmas;
- Want to be seen to be fair;
- Communicate results to staff;
- Provide safe, supportive environments;
- Provide professional development that is relevant to staff needs;
- Apply new understandings, knowledge, and skills they have learned; and
- Have high expectations of students.

In summary, the common features of successful leadership in schools in high-poverty communities have been found to include the cooperation and alignment of others to shared vision and values, distributed leadership, a core belief that all children can learn and achieve irrespective of context or background, targeted staff development, and relationship and community building (Bishop, 1999; Harris & Chapman, 2002, 2004). The core message about successful leadership in schools facing challenging circumstances is one of building capacity through empowering, involving, and developing others, and by providing systems of learning support, guidance, and assistance.

Conclusion

Schools operating in contexts of disadvantage have levels of performance that, in most cases, fall short of national averages. This not only presents them with a range of practical difficulties, but it also asks a great deal of those who lead the school to buck this particular trend. There is little doubt that it would be simpler to pass off responsibility to other sectors or to governments and claim there is little that such schools can do. Similarly, it is easier to diminish any school improvement efforts as "naïve . . . with no sense of the structural, the political, and the historical as constraints" (Grace, 1984, p. xii) than to attempt to assist schools with strategies and approaches that could help their teachers and students. As Stoll and Myers (1998) note, there are no quick fixes for schools facing challenging circumstances, but there is an emerging base of evidence suggesting that leadership is a powerful determinant of school performance and subsequent educational success.

The research evidence concerning improving schools in difficult contexts demonstrates that each school within this grouping exhibits a unique organizational mix of cultural typology, improvement trajectory, and level of effectiveness. Unlike effective schools, which have been shown to exhibit similar characteristics to each other, schools in the low-performing grouping may look superficially homogeneous, but in practice they exhibit very different combinations of characteristics. Therefore, it seems important that any improvement efforts consider more highly differentiated and context-specific programs of intervention (Harris & Chapman, 2004).

While there seems to be a general recognition of a need to move toward more context-specific forms of intervention and improvement in challenged schools, the necessary changes are simply not coming quickly enough. Initiatives come and go without knowledge transfer or knowledge building. Each new initiative starts as if previous attempts had never existed. Achieving contextually specific school improvement will require a radical shift away from short-term approaches to change, standardized school improvement approaches, and externally driven agendas.

The bond between social class and educational achievement is a particularly powerful one, and particularly resistant to change. Breaking this bond will require leadership that is responsive to school context and is underpinned by an unrelenting focus on improving conditions at the building and classroom levels. The research highlights that successful leaders in SFCC are constantly managing tensions and problems directly related to the particular circumstances and context of the school. The main leadership task facing them is one of coping with unpredictability, conflict, and dissent on a daily basis without discarding their moral purpose and core values. Successful leaders of schools in difficulty tend to be, above all, people-centered, combining a willingness to be collaborative with the desire to promote the highest levels of teaching and learning. The evidence suggests that while the challenges facing such leaders are considerable, the personal and professional benefits far outweigh them. We need to highlight those benefits if we are to ensure that there is a continuity of capable leadership in our most difficult schools.

Successful leaders of schools in difficulty tend to be, above all, people-centered, combining a willingness to be collaborative with the desire to promote the highest levels of teaching and learning.

As the long-term pattern of educational inequality seems very likely to persist, schools facing challenging circumstances must look for an approach to intervention that ensures a fit between the developmental stage and growth state of the school and the improvement strategies employed. This will require careful diagnosis and an appropriate selection of strategies that best match the prevailing conditions that vary within such schools. It will also require leaders with a strong sense of moral purpose and a firm belief that schools and young people can achieve against all odds, and that high educational achievement is an aspiration for the many rather than the few.

References

Bishop, P. (1999). School-based trust in Victoria: Some telling lessons. *Australian Journal of Education, 43*(3), 273–284.

Blackmore, J. (1999). *Troubling women: Feminism, leadership, and educational change.* Buckingham, UK: Open University Press.

Borman, G., D'Agostino, J., Wong, K., & Hedges, L. (1998). The longitudinal achievement of Chapter 1 students: Preliminary evidence from the Prospects Study. *Journal of Education for Students Placed at Risk, 3*(4), 363–399.

Day, C., Sammons, P., Leithwood, K., Harris, A., & Hopkins, D. (2009). *The impact of leadership on pupil outcomes: Final report.* London: Department for Children, Schools and Families.

Equalities Review. (2007). *Fairness and freedom: The final report of the Equalities Review.* London: Her Majesty's Stationery Office. Available at http://archive.cabinetoffice.gov.uk/equalitiesreview.

Feinstein, L. (2000). *The relative economic importance of academic, psychological, and behavioural attributes developed in childhood* (Research Paper 443). London: Centre for Economic Performance, London School of Economics and Political Science.

Fullan, M. (2006). *Turnaround leadership.* San Francisco: Jossey-Bass.

Grace, G. (1984). *Education in the city.* London: Routledge/Kegan Paul.

Gray, J. (2000). *Causing concern but improving: A review of schools' experience.* London: Department for Education and Employment.

Gray, J. (2001). Building for improvement and sustaining change in schools serving disadvantaged communities. In M. Maden (Ed.), *Success against the odds—Five years on* (pp. 1–39). London: RoutledgeFalmer.

Gray, J. (2004). Frames of reference and traditions of interpretation: Some issues in the identification of "under-achieving" schools. *British Journal of Educational Studies, 52*(3), 293–309.

Harris, A. (2002). *Leadership in schools facing challenging circumstances.* Paper presented at the International Congress of School Effectiveness and School Improvement, Copenhagen, Denmark.

Harris, A. (2007, July). Distributed leadership: Conceptual confusion and empirical reticence. *International Journal of Leadership in Education, 10*(3), 1–11.

Harris, A., & Chapman, C. (2002). *Effective leadership in schools facing challenging circumstances.* Nottingham, UK: National College for School Leadership. Available at http://www.ncsl.org.uk/research.

Harris, A., & Chapman, C. (2004). Towards differentiated improvement for schools in challenging circumstances. *British Journal of Educational Studies, 52*(4).

Harris, A., Clarke, P., James, S., Harris, B., & Gunraj, J. (2006). *Improving schools in difficulty.* London: Continuum Press.

Harris, A., Muijs, D., Chapman, C., Stoll, L., & Russ, J. (2003). *Raising attainment in the former coalfield areas.* Moorfoot, Sheffield, UK: Department for Education and Skills.

Hopkins, D. (2001). *Meeting the challenge: An improvement guide for schools facing challenging circumstances.* London: Department for Education and Skills.

Knapp, M. S. (2001). Policy, poverty and capable teaching. In B. Biddle (Ed.), *Social class, poverty, and education.* New York: RoutledgeFalmer.

Leithwood, K., Day, C., Sammons, P., Harris, A., & Hopkins, D. (2007). *Leadership and student learning outcomes: Interim report.* London: Department for Children, Schools and Families.

Leithwood, K., & Jantzi, D. (2000). The effects of transformational leadership on organisational conditions and student engagement. *Journal of Educational Administration, 38*(2), 112–129.

Leithwood, K., & Steinbach, R. (2002). *Successful leadership for especially challenging schools.* Unpublished paper, Ontario Institute for Studies in Education, University of Toronto.

Maden, M. (Ed.). (2001). *Success against the odds—five years on: Revisiting effective schools in disadvantaged areas.* London: Routledge.

Mortimore, P. (1993). School effectiveness and the management of effective learning and teaching. *School Effectiveness and School Improvement, 4*(4), 290–310.

Mulford, B., Kendall, B., Edmunds, B., Kendall, L., Ewington, J., & Silins, H. (2007). Successful school leadership: What and who decides. *Australian Journal of Education, 51*(3).

Power, S., Warren, S., Gillbourn, D., Clark, A., Thomas, S., & Kelly, C. (2003). *Education in deprived areas: Outcomes, inputs, and processes.* London: Institute of Education, University of London.

Rainwater, L., & Smeeding, T. (2003). *Poor kids in a rich country: America's children in comparative perspective.* New York: Russell Sage Foundation.

Reynolds, D., Clarke, P., & Harris, A. (2004, April 11–16). *Challenging the challenged: Improving schools in exceptionally challenging circumstances.* Paper presented at the annual conference of the American Educational Research Association, San Diego.

Reynolds, D., Hopkins, D., Potter, D., & Chapman, C. (2001). *School improvement for schools facing challenging circumstances: A review of research and practice.* London: Department for Education and Skills.

Stoll, L., Fink, D., & Earl, L. (2003). *It's about learning (and it's about time).* London: RoutledgeFalmer.

Stoll, L., & Myers, K. (1998). *No quick fixes: Perspectives on schools in difficulty.* London: Falmer Press.

Teese, R. (2000). *Academic success and social power.* Melbourne, Australia: Melbourne University Press.

Thomson, P., & Harris, A. (2004). *Leading schools that serve neighbourhoods and communities in poverty.* Paper presented at the Second International Leadership in Education Research Network Meeting, Boston.

Townsend, T. (Ed.). (2007). *International handbook of school effectiveness and improvement.* Dordrecht, The Netherlands: Springer.

Van Velzen, W., Miles, M., Elholm, M., Hameyer, U., & Robin, D. (1985). *Making school improvement work.* Leuven, Belgium: Acco.

West, M., Jackson, D., Harris, A., & Hopkins, D. (2000). Leadership for school improvement. In K. Riley & K. Seashore Louis (Eds.), *Leadership for change.* London: RoutledgeFalmer.

CHAPTER SEVEN

DEVELOPING LEADERS OF LEARNERS

ROBERT W. KATULAK

Leadership in the 21st century can no longer adhere to the paradigm of leadership that prevailed 10 or 15 years ago. The heightened sense of accountability in education today—as well as the increased social, emotional, and academic needs of the students we serve—make it logical and necessary that we develop a more extensive, embracing conception of leadership.

Leadership must be shared; it can no longer reside solely in the hands of a superintendent or a building principal. Leadership must reside in the hands of our teachers. We can no longer be a "sage on the stage," but now must serve as a "guide on the side." In this chapter, I'll explore many ways in which we can move an organization—whether it be a school building or an entire school system—forward, in order to meet the increased needs of our clients: our students. In order to do this, we now must accept the charge of creating *leaders of learners* from within our organizations. Teachers are the true leaders in the classroom; when they engage students in meaningful and creative ways, students will follow their lead. A teacher's craft of leadership is often the difference between high academic achievement and below-proficiency performance.

We now must accept the charge of creating leaders of learners from within our organizations.

Such a journey can only be successful when it begins at the grassroots level. A shared mission or vision is absolutely necessary for buy-in. Teachers, through their united organizations or unions, must be empowered to feel in control of the programs that they are expected to embrace and implement, in order to increase student academic achievement. Robert Marzano's (2007) research indicates that the principal is the major change agent in a school; however, principals are only as effective as the teachers who are charged with the task of implementing new programs within the four walls of their classrooms. The principal's role must transform to truly develop leaders of learners in classrooms. This is how the paradigm must shift to implement and sustain all innovations in education today.

Change begins with research and data analysis, which must be conducted by our teachers. Here is where the superintendent or the building principal becomes the mentor, or the guide on the side. This person's role is to train teachers to use research and data-analysis protocols to understand how best to reach students. Teachers must use current brain research, such as the work of Eric Jensen (2001), Pat Wolfe (2001), and Caine and Caine (1991), to develop pedagogy that effectively reaches every student.

Research in learning styles and reading styles points to the necessity of teaching students according to the modality preference most suited to their needs. All students flourish in instructional environments that are geared to different abilities and interests. According to Marie Carbo (2007),

> Differentiated instruction is most powerful when students' strengths and interests are both identified and accommodated, especially their global/analytic styles and perceptual strengths. (p. 61)

Although students might not know directly about learning and reading styles, they are quite aware of the fact that teacher leaders who employ these strategies are the same ones who don't continue blindly forward when students don't comprehend material the first time they're exposed to it. Leaders of learners understand how to transform students' lives. They know that teachers must learn to teach differently to reach those students who may not be reached right away. Leaders know that in order to reach their students, they must find ways to connect subjects to students by linking to whatever is important and interesting to them. A few examples of strategies schools can use to accomplish this goal are described below. These were among the suggestions and procedures I implemented as assistant superintendent for elementary and middle-level education in the Haverstraw-Stony Point Central School District in Rockland County in New York State.

Each semester, district or building administrators can truly become guides on the side, providing resources to teachers by conducting *professional book talks*. Administrators can facilitate this process by actually buying the professional resource books, the materials, and—this matters!—refreshments for the time the teachers meet to discuss the books they've read. Refreshments represent a minimal expenditure—whether it be a continental breakfast with coffee, bagels, and juice (if the meeting is scheduled before school), or cookies, punch, and crackers and cheese for an after-school meeting—but teachers will very much appreciate this gesture. The administrator can facilitate the discussion by providing protocols or an occasional guided question in the manner of a Socratic seminar. One important thing to remember is that the research should not be frivolous, but rather should be connected to what teachers want and what they realize will be beneficial to their everyday instruction. Teachers appreciate useful research that can be turned around and implemented in classrooms within 48 hours.

Another strategy to accomplish this goal is the creation of a *collegial circle* in each school. Each circle would have a "turnkey leader" who would be in charge (and who would receive an annual stipend for this). The turnkey model is grounded in the premise that members from the teaching ranks volunteer to assume the role of a leader of learners. These turnkey leaders, following the business model, turn the "key" of information over to the "owners" of the building (the teachers) upon completion of staff development. The turnkey concept means that certain individuals who possess leadership traits can be trained in procedures of teaching group-facilitation skills and the mechanics of creating a product or outcome.

An example of this would be teaching the process of curriculum mapping and then actually creating a yearlong science curriculum map. The turnkey leaders are *designated by their peers* in each grade level or building to act as their leader of learners. These peer-appointed leaders of learners need to be well respected so that their fellow teachers are willing to follow their lead. These individuals are given the time to be trained by administrators in the appropriate

———————— ✂ ————————

Peer-appointed leaders of learners need to be well respected so that their fellow teachers are willing to follow their lead.

protocols, and are sent for staff development and professional conferences to build their capacity. The turnkey person assumes the responsibility of taking all the information and knowledge back to the building and teaching others in the designated group to build their capacity in any given subject.

In tight budgetary times, many districts can no longer afford middle-level management positions such as assistant principals or assistant superintendents; as a result, these leaders of learners can play an integral role in sustaining the momentum of innovations. In order to survive in times of high accountability and tight budgets, administrators are finding that they must work smarter rather than harder in order to be effective. We can no longer view district or building administrators as superheroes, ready to leap over big problems in a single bound by themselves. True leaders build the capacity of others to continually develop and expand the critical mass of leaders of learners.

As one vitally important example, literacy permeates (or *should* permeate) all content areas in today's schools. Every state in the United States, under the watchful eye of No Child Left Behind, is held accountable for assessing student proficiency in the areas of English language arts, mathematics, science, and in some cases social studies. Each and every educator realizes from day one that every content-area assessment is an assessment of literacy skills. To build student capacity for excellence, we must constantly build teacher capacity in instructional pedagogy as it relates to the skills that bring about literacy.

One turnkey model that is extremely practical and effective in this regard is the institution of a *literacy reading coach*. Every district should consider creating a minimum of one literacy coach per building, at every level. The job of these coaches is to serve as the leader of learners in the domain of literacy; they can serve in a dual position as teacher developer/coach and as a remedial instructor if budgetary restrictions make it necessary. This literacy coach works to build the skills of classroom teachers in best practices that will enhance vocabulary and comprehension.

This is not a random plan, however. The art of teaching is also a science, as Marzano reminds us in *The Art and Science of Teaching* (2007):

If a teacher does not have the correct mixture of effective instructional strategies, effective classroom management strategies and effective classroom curriculum design, the science experiences in the classroom will negatively explode. (p. 5)

Teachers need to follow the medical model—analyzing, diagnosing, prescribing, implementing, monitoring, and evaluating the methods they choose to implement in the classroom on a daily basis. Higher education does not adequately provide new teachers with the full range of instructional strategies they'll require in order to meet the diverse learning needs of their students. Quite often, new and even veteran teachers are hard-pressed to define accurately what a balanced literacy approach to reading is. A literacy coach becomes the "ad hoc" college professor to develop other leaders of learners by providing them with the theory and research of balanced literacy. Then literacy coaches provide modeling and guided and individual practice for teachers so that these techniques become part of their daily repertoire.

The whole concept of the link between fluency and comprehension skills, for example, is often absent from a teacher's "bag of tricks." Literacy coaches develop the skills of leaders of learners by providing assistance in learning, implementing, and monitoring commercial programs such as Marie Carbo's Power Pak Reading, Read Naturally, Scholastic's Read 180, and the Six-Minute Solution by Gail Adams and Sheron Brown, all of which address the link between fluency and comprehension. Equipped with the knowledge base of each of these fluency strategies, teachers can make informed decisions as to what works best for each individual or group of students, fully cognizant that there is no one magic pill for every student.

We can no longer assume that teachers know how to differentiate instruction within a 90-minute literacy period. Leaders of learners must use direct instruction to assist their colleagues in understanding the use of flexible, fluid group instruction. They need help in learning how to create, monitor, and maintain student involvement at centers, and how to use formative assessment on an ongoing basis. It is essential that leaders of learners use the coaching model of assistance, so that all teachers feel comfortable taking risks to acquire new skills.

At the secondary level, literacy coaches become even more critical than at the elementary level. We all realize that by Grade 7, academic content takes over and teachers are no longer teaching the art or science of learning to read. Students at this level are now reading to learn content about five times more often than they were required to do in elementary school—and yet there is no one really available to help them in this endeavor.

Literacy coaches play an essential role at the secondary level by building the capacity of teachers through modeling practices and instructing them in how to teach reading skills across the content areas. Laura Robb, in *Teaching Reading in Social Studies, Science, and Math* (2003), states,

> It is essential for secondary teachers to take short bursts of time each day to teach reading and learning strategies that will help their students "unlock" every kind of text and thus experience success with every subject. (p. 7)

Science or social studies teachers can no longer say, "I'm not a reading teacher, so that's not my job." Right now, most teachers at the secondary level feel ill-prepared to teach reading skills. Content literacy continues to be the complaint of every secondary teacher: "If students can't read the textbook, how can I be expected to teach them the content?" The answer is this: Leaders of learners can show the way, using the same nonfiction material that teachers use on a daily basis.

Literacy coaches usually are successful in the development of leaders of learners regarding instructional strategies, but they have a somewhat greater challenge when it comes to building a new paradigm for assessment. Leaders of learners subscribe to the belief and vision that we must constantly be monitoring student progress by keeping our finger on the pulse of whether or not our students "get" whatever is being taught. Richard and Becky DuFour, in *Whatever It Takes* (2004), make the point that it is no longer acceptable to cling to the belief that "I taught it and they just didn't learn it." In their chapter "How Do We Respond When Kids Don't Learn?" they state that in order to accomplish this goal, "A school will develop consistent, systematic procedures

Leaders of learners subscribe to the belief and vision that we must constantly be monitoring student progress by keeping our finger on the pulse of whether or not our students "get" whatever is being taught.

that ensure each student is guaranteed additional time and support when needed."

In a professional learning community, leaders of learners understand and are committed to the premise that some students require additional time, resources, and support beyond the school day or year if they are to learn all the standards. When this need occurs, teachers adjust their schedules accordingly. This ability to adapt is not something that teachers acquire by osmosis, however; it must be cultivated by leaders of learners so there is grassroots support for such an attitudinal change. There must be a systemic response that answers three basic questions:

1. What do I want my students to learn? (State standards)

2. How do I know whether or not they learned it? (Formative assessments)

3. What do I do when they have not learned it the first time? (Differentiation)

If we want this process to work, we must apply our turnkey model to assessment as well. Turnkey teachers in each content area work together across grade levels to create collaborative, teacher-made, multi-modality assessments that continually assess at benchmark points, whether or not students have mastered the standards and objectives. It is at that point, when these formative assessments are administered and scored, that the turnkey teachers bring together groups of teachers to analyze data and discuss alternate ways to differentiate for reteaching the material.

This is where we once again have a paradigm shift in how we do school! Understand that the concept of leaders of learners can often be synonymous with turnkey leaders when it comes to specific strategies being taught to others. However, the term *leaders of learners* is more generally applied to all educators who are charged with the mission of facilitating the strategies that help their students acquire knowledge. Leaders of learners then need to shift into a different gear in order to make possible various alternative ways of teaching that are not just slower or louder methods, but truly differentiate instruction to match students' stylistic preferences.

One critical area that requires additional attention is the development of leaders of learners in the area of mathematics in both elementary and middle schools. Throughout the history of American education, we have had teachers at this level who are "math-phobic" because they themselves were not good math students when they were in school, or because they have had little or no professional preparation for the teaching of math concepts. As the United States loses ground to India, China, and Japan in a global economy (as measured by proficiency based on the recent Trends in International Mathematics and Science Study [TIMSS] study; see http://nces.ed .gov/timss), it is essential for us to strengthen our teachers' knowledge base, which will directly influence our students' understanding of this complex subject.

Here, more than in any other area of the curriculum, it is critical that we create the positions of math specialists as leaders of learners. Ideally, teachers in these positions will have certification in the teaching of mathematics or have a concentration of math credits. Math specialists are pivotal in assisting noncertified math teachers who are assigned the task of teaching math in Grades 3 through 6 in obtaining a thorough understanding of not only the *content* math standards but also the *process* math standards.

These math specialists are the equivalent of a major league sports coach. They are charged with a variety of tasks to develop classroom instructional leaders. To begin with, they must be knowledgeable of all facets of the state mathematics standards and also be fully informed regarding the components of whatever district math program is being used to teach those standards. They must be the turnkey cheerleaders, with a secure knowledge base, who are able to sell the curriculum and align all standards and assessments. They must be the go-to person from whom a new (or a veteran) teacher can seek advice regarding initial lesson instruction or reteaching ideas when students may not have mastered the material the first time out of the gate. They are the pacemakers or schedulers who plot out the curriculum math lesson on a time line, whether manually or through the use of an electronic curriculum mapping tool such as Rubicon Atlas.

These math specialists must be leaders of learners who take the initiative to "courageously abandon" those items in the teacher's edition that any given unit can do without. The math specialist must also be the person who houses all manipulatives for hands-on differentiated learning and who can send a teacher to a virtual manipulative website if necessary. The math specialist turnkey is the person who attends the statewide mathematics conference or represents the district at the National Council of Teacher of Mathematics (NCTM) conference each year.

The person in this position must be able to build the storehouse of mathematical strategies for teachers, in the same way as the reading or literacy coaches. This individual must be able to teach and model strategies for alternate pathways of instruction found in such works as *Alternative Math Techniques When Nothing Else Seems to Work,* by Richard Cooper (2005), or *Take It to the* Mat, by David Thiel (2006). (These programs clearly show ways in which math specialists can educate other leaders of learners in how to teach traditional mathematical strategies that students have difficulty grasping.) Whatever the case, these leaders of learners become the major support for teachers in need of assistance.

The final group of turnkey leaders of learners is made up of the traditional committee chairs or department chairs. These key people, who must have the respect of their peers, facilitate monthly department or vertical team meetings in a subject area. They become part of a superintendent's or assistant superintendent's monthly cabinet meetings wherein curriculum concerns and innovations are planned, discussed, and moved forward for implementation at the building level. They work with teams of teachers in a nonjudgmental, nonevaluative climate to re-create the model of analyze, diagnose, prescribe, implement, remediate, and evaluate. They often represent the district at regional and statewide meetings as conduits of information for future skills building, which in turn improves students' academic success in the areas that they represent.

It's hard to overstate the necessity of peer review and acceptance of all initiatives if we're to be successful in sustaining important and necessary changes. (It's also important, by the way, to keep union leaders "in the loop" at all times.) The committee chairs would have the important role of keeping teachers informed of all joint decisions at faculty meetings. They would also be the leaders of learners at the 2-hour-per-month staff development time that districts could build into contracts to enable teachers to grow professionally. They are awarded staff in-service hours, which would

It's hard to overstate the necessity of peer review and acceptance of all initiatives if we're to be successful in sustaining important and necessary changes.

count toward increased in-service credit in the form of salary adjustment upon accumulation of 15 hours. This salary adjustment would remain for the duration of their employment as chair.

One final area that needs to be discussed is the possibility that leaders inside an organization may lack specific knowledge regarding a problem, and the school district may need to seek the expertise of leaders from outside the organization. In such a case, a different means of transmitting knowledge would need to be applied. A case in point was our district's being cited for a 405 citation (a state audit of the special education program); in our case, we were told that we had an overrepresentation of children of color being classified as special education students and placed in the most restrictive special education settings. No one on the district staff possessed the knowledge, research background, or expertise necessary to develop the capacity of all learners in this regard. Consequently, the district entered into a partnership with the Metropolitan Urban Studies Division at New York University to develop leaders of learners in two major areas: (1) teaching Latino and African American males, and (2) culturally responsive teaching techniques.

For our district, a positive side effect of the creation of a pool of leaders of learners was the creation of pre-referral strategies for special education needs. The district created a Pyramid of Interventions (see Figure 7.1) that addressed the response to intervention (RtI) requirement by New York State and provided assistance to all schools in reducing referrals and lowering the percentage of students of color who were slated to be classified. The designated cohort of leaders became empowered with alternate ways of serving special needs students without the necessity of classifying them. Within 2 years' time, this training produced a 3 percent reduction in the number of students of color who were classified.

The Haverstraw-Stony Point Consolidated School District now makes it a priority that turnkey leaders keep this issue of overclassifying children of color into special education on the front burner, and they are examining methods of declassifying existing special education students in an inclusive, welcoming environment. Many of the classified students of color happened to be males, and an outgrowth of this work resulted in the need to incorporate more kinesthetic activities in day-to-day instruction, which aligned itself perfectly to work done in the district that was grounded in Marie Carbo's (2007) research. Many males of color have diagnosed learning

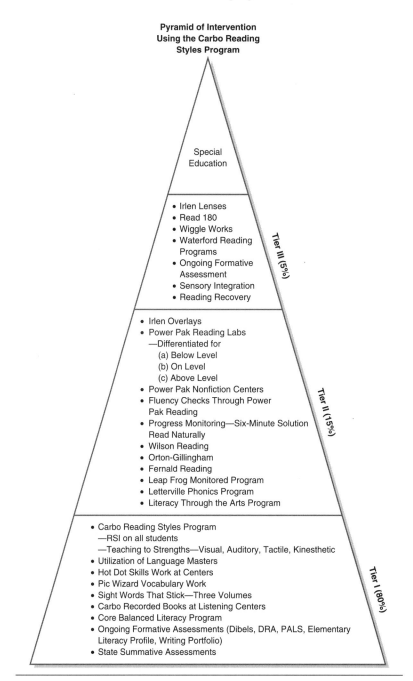

Figure 7.1   Pyramid of Interventions Using the Carbo Reading Styles Program

styles that register a preference for learning by doing and moving. Traditional classroom instruction tends to be "chalk and talk"—in other words, a visual and auditory instructional approach that does not meet the styles of these students, causing them to turn off to instruction and fall further behind in mastering state standards. As a result, as the gap grows wider, these students are referred to special education and are classified at a greater rate than their white counterparts.

The district is well on its way in reducing the percentage of students of color who are classified compared to the district classification rate for all students. The percentage of students of color who are classified compared to the previous high of 14 percent is down to 11 percent.

Leaders must come to realize that their efforts are sustainable only if the vision that drives them is acceptable to those in the ranks. Leaders of learners, once taught what is important and how to implement change, must also be taught how to monitor and evaluate innovations so they continue to produce the desired results each year.

If change and innovation are to be sustained, research clearly states that all efforts must be rooted in visionary, strategic styles of leadership. Leaders must come to realize that their efforts are sustainable only if the vision that drives them is acceptable to those in the ranks. Leaders of learners, once taught what is important and how to implement change, must also be taught how to monitor and evaluate innovations so they continue to produce the desired results each year. This works best when central office staff—including the superintendent and the assistant superintendents for curriculum and instruction—model the desired behaviors for the leaders of learners. *This preparation bears fruit when leaders climb down from their ivory towers and lead alongside rather than from above.*

A 5-year plan aligned to the district vision must be strategically laid out with all stakeholders in the district. Mechanisms that provide technical assistance in the classroom for all teachers are developed from the premise that teacher coaches and administrators are trained first, and then they transmit their knowledge to stakeholders. Then, most important, these teachers assume the role of provider of technical assistance for continued implementation.

This technical assistance can take many different forms. Mentors can provide technical assistance by first becoming experts themselves; then they can create a technical assistance calendar wherein every 2 weeks they observe the implementation of a given strategy and offer precise, concise constructive feedback to move the initiative forward. This feedback might range from minor suggestions about a classroom management transition technique to something as consequential as how to conduct a parent-teacher conference with a belligerent parent.

Note that this approach has been around for many years under the guise of peer coaching. The subtle difference here is that the district invests heavily in these leaders of learners by sending them to national conferences and seminars to allow them to stay current in their knowledge base regarding specific innovations.

Here is another example: The Haverstraw-Stony Point School District created a strategic model for the implementation of Developing Reading Styles Model Schools, based on the work of Marie Carbo's National Reading Styles Institute. When I served in Haverstraw-Stony Point as assistant superintendent of curriculum and instruction, I worked collaboratively with teachers and administrators to identify schools in need of improvement. Entire schools in this large district were offered the opportunity to work toward the status of Reading Styles Model School.

Schools volunteered for this program, and we adopted a model of technical assistance. Each school year I trained cohorts of 25 teachers per semester in Carbo's Reading Styles Model. All staff involved in the training received 3 full days of staff development regarding the applicable research. Materials and instructional strategies necessary to implement the program were provided as part of the training. In between the days of training, I planned a schedule of classroom observations and technical assistance to determine the fidelity and the impact of the strategies being implemented. After each technical assistance visit, I gave a report of constructive suggestions to the teachers with a nonevaluative, face-to-face conference on how to fine-tune the implemented strategies. Assistance was also given on how to manage students' use of program materials or components.

In the final session, as a bit of icing on the cake, participants saw themselves transformed into leaders of learners when they demonstrated a technique or shared a material, game, or center they had created to sustain the program. In addition to the three technical assistance visits, every participant walked away with 24 additional suggestions.

Once all staff members had been trained, further technical assistance was provided by the building principal and me to ensure consistency in the implementation of strategies, materials, and management tools. Some of the additional technical assistance suggestions included the standardization of color-coded directions with pictures that gave a step-by-step process for students to follow at each literacy or math center. Another fine-tuning point was the placement of certain materials in the room for easy access and accountability. Materials such as electro-boards, flip-chutes, pic-a-hole cards, and wrap-ups all help students to stay focused on, and accountable for, lesson objectives.

As leaders of learners, each principal and I also developed a mechanism for the production of classroom manipulatives, learning centers, and Carbo recorded stories. This system entailed what we called "give to get." "Town hall meetings" were held for two periods prior to a grade-level teacher's prep period. During that 90-minute block, the teachers worked together to create materials as a grade level. Also during the 90 minutes, the building principal and I would conduct the town hall meeting with an entire grade level—possibly 200 students—during which they would cover the Pillars of Character Education or have an assembly on citizenship.

District standards continued to improve, and teachers were treated as professionals and given the opportunity to work collaboratively and work "smarter," rather than just harder and harder. The last fine-tuning suggestion involved getting ready for evaluation of the model schools by focusing on the presentation and organization of classrooms. Evidence of students' work and mastery of the tasks related to all four modalities of learning were on display, ranging from color-coded mind maps to videos showing the retelling of a story students performed in a Reader's Theater production. Although consistency became the expected norm, creativity still overflowed in each classroom.

DATA DRIVES INSTRUCTIONAL
FOCUS FOR LEADERS OF LEARNERS

The issue of strategic planning becomes crucial in times of crisis. Under NCLB, many districts, due to the complexity of the needs of their students, were identified as schools in need of improvement because of the performance of a designated subgroup. Most often, these subgroups consisted of English language learners, special education students, free and reduced-price lunch students, or a combination of any of these groups. For the first time, even high-performing schools ended up on state lists because of an identifiable subgroup.

This unique challenge spotlighted the need for additional technical assistance and for the development of a new group of leaders of learners called the "data team" in the West Haverstraw District. Under the leadership of the district instructional leaders (the assistant superintendents of curriculum and instruction), each school created a team of three to five members, including a parent, to become the data team. They were charged with being trained in examining root causes for instructional gaps, looking for academic symptoms that needed to be addressed and ways of implementing research-based strategies that would address the learning needs of all identified subgroups. (In reality, all of these tasks would increase the academic performance of all students.)

With a school improvement template providing a roadmap for direction, these data teams began their work by examining state and district test results, classroom and program test results, and classroom beliefs and practices. It was at this point that the visionary element of strategic planning took center stage. If the schools truly believed that all students could and would learn if taught according to their identified reading style, then it was up to the district administration to put their money where their mouth was. After being trained in the analysis of test data, the staff took ownership of the data and the goals. Armed with this information, staff development needs were identified on a district level and supported with additional staff development at the building level. The staff development topics were chosen by the District Planning Team, not by the central office.

In 3 years, the district went from having six schools identified as being in need of improvement to six schools identified as "High-Achieving/Gap-Closing Schools." This achievement would not have been possible if the only leader of learners had been the building

———————— ✥ ————————

In 3 years, the Haverstraw-Stony Point District went from having six schools identified as being in need of improvement to six schools identified as "High-Achieving/Gap-Closing Schools." This achievement would not have been possible if the only leader of learners had been the building principal in each school.

principal in each school. This honor was won through the shared strategic and visionary leadership of the members of the data teams, who had truly become leaders of learners.

In many school districts, the primary instructional focus is the subject area of literacy. In the Haverstraw-Stony Point Consolidated School District, however, there was a different need. Analyzing state test data, the data teams discovered the district was hemorrhaging in the areas of fourth- and eighth-grade mathematics results. With an understanding that this was clearly unacceptable—due to our belief system that all students can and will learn if taught according to their learning styles—a task force of stakeholders was created to address this problem.

The first issue to be addressed was the apparent lack of leaders of learners in the area of mathematics from kindergarten through Grade 7. Math specialists, who were already in place, spearheaded an intervention plan to stop the bleeding. Curriculum materials and textbook programs were examined for content and alignment to state standards. This examination revealed a disconnect between the two, so the math specialists worked with task force members to research, examine, and solicit presentations from companies that met the identified need. Teacher leaders were then invited to be part of a process of building capacity and knowledge in mathematics through in-service staff development while also piloting programs and materials.

Once again, the district, putting its money where its mouth was, built in professional planning days (monthly) and after-school teaming hours (including stipends for participants) to build a cadre of leaders of learners at every grade level in every school. These teachers became the go-to people, along with the building administrators and math specialist, to apply the tourniquets and stop the bleeding. At the end of the year, a standards-based program was selected, and then the next phase of the strategic plan was implemented. Training of all staff in the use of the program and the creation of manipulatives was provided. Grade-level leaders of learners held monthly staff development days, selecting assessment monitoring time lines and creating and stockpiling hands-on manipulatives to implement the program. The critical mass of teachers who could do what was needed was expanded and trained. At the end of the first year, math scores indicated proficiency levels had increased by 10 percent in Grade 4 and 6 percent in Grade 8 based on state assessments.

The next year brought additional challenges related to meeting the needs of the district's English language learners. Targeted staff development in differentiated strategies designed for these students was provided through New York State's regular and special education regional consortium and by using consultant services regarding Math Linkages (a planned format for reteaching math), as they related to the district's vision and strategic plan. Staff members were given a set of alternative strategies to use with students who had language deficiencies so they could still progress with their math skills. The Total Physical Response methodology, which was compatible with the district's emphasis on a tactile-kinesthetic exposure to learning, was employed to reach out to these students, as had been suggested by the New York State Bilingual Education Technical Assistance Consortium. Slowly but surely, these students responded, and they met their adequate yearly progress benchmark in mathematics by the end of the year.

CONCLUSION

Looking to the future in education at all levels, strategic planning is certainly a key component for ensuring its survival. Shared leadership is now a paramount need of any effective organization, and it must be timely, competitive, and technology based. Spreadsheets, data-analysis charts, and graphs must become everyday tools in our work.

The final challenge we needed to face in West Haverstraw was the infusion of technology across the grades and across the curriculum. These days, technology produces a great divide between the *digital immigrants* (those of us over the age of, say, 45 who did not grow up with technology) and the *digital natives*—our students and younger staff—for whom technology is a way of life.

Once again, the leaders of learners model played a critical role in helping us to embed technology into everyday teaching practices. Teacher leaders become turnkey staff developers in assisting staff of all ages in using the Internet as an instructional tool; using virtual manipulatives in a math class; taking a virtual field trip to the battlefields of the Civil War; and using a SMART Board for instruction, note taking, and interactive communication in all subjects.

Change is an ongoing process, not an isolated event, when it comes to motivation regarding technology. Teachers embraced the use of technology when shown how to do so by their peers in a manner that was nonthreatening and immediately useful. Teachers and students were thrilled to participate in a videoconferencing project called Living Historians. The ability to see and talk to Amelia Earhart, Mark Twain, Thomas Edison, Orville Wright, Benjamin Franklin, or NASA astronauts brought history alive. It was truly the "icing on the cake" of teaching.

In the final analysis, we in leadership roles need to begin to delegate our decision-making powers to the leaders of learners using the turnkey model. We understand that the road to academic success cannot be reached by only one driver. The mark of success for any leader is if his or her work is sustained after the leader leaves an organization. A true leader knows that if he or she models shared leadership correctly, other leaders will know how to imitate this model. After all, imitation is the sincerest form of flattery.

REFERENCES

Caine, R., & Caine, G. (1991). *Making connections: Teaching and the human brain.* Alexandria, VA: Association for Supervision and Curriculum Development.

Carbo, M. (2007). *Becoming a great teacher of reading.* Thousand Oaks, CA: Corwin.

Cooper, R. (2005). *Alternative math techniques when nothing else seems to work.* Longmont, CO: Sopris West.

DuFour, R., & DuFour, B. (2004). *Whatever it takes.* Bloomington, IN: Solution Tree.

Jensen, E. (2001). *Arts with the brain in mind.* Alexandria, VA: Association for Supervision and Curriculum Development.

Marzano, R. (2007). *The art and science of teaching: A comprehensive framework for effective instruction.* Alexandria, VA: Association for Supervision and Curriculum Development.

Robb, L. (2003). *Teaching reading in social studies, science, and math.* New York: Scholastic.

Thiel, D. (2006). *Take it to the mat.* Las Vegas: Southern Nevada Regional Professional Development Program.

Wolfe, P. (2001). *Brain matters: Translating research into classroom practice.* Alexandria, VA: Association for Supervision and Curriculum Development.

CHAPTER EIGHT

BUILDING LEADERSHIP CAPACITY FOR SCHOOL-BASED SOCIAL-EMOTIONAL LEARNING (SEL)

The Trajectory of Young Leaders

MAURICE J. ELIAS

With Victoria Blakeney, Anchorage, Alaska, Public Schools;
Paul Flaspohler, Miami University;
Melissa A. Reeves, Cherry Creek School District, Colorado;
and Jennifer Vargo, Ohio Department of Education

I ndividuals are typically studied as leaders after their qualifications have been well established. At times, they will reflect on the road they traveled to get to their leadership position and will elaborate their leadership philosophy. Much has been learned from these accounts, and the literature on leadership, especially in the schools, is growing exponentially. Sometimes, however, it is possible to study leaders at an earlier point in their career trajectory, when their leadership qualities are just being recognized. This chapter represents such an opportunity, in a distinctly school-based context.

In the 1990s, a consortium of leaders in the field of school-based action research related to the promotion of social competence was established (Elias et al., 1996). This group consisted of individuals who, for the most part, had their own independent research teams, school-based social competence promotion programs, and projects. While there was a great deal of mutual respect and occasional collaboration, the participants generally followed a university academic model emphasizing individual accomplishment and recognition. Over time, these individuals expressed growing concern about the failure of schools to implement the best of what was known about social and emotional development and the prevention of problem behaviors. They felt there was a significant and continuing gap between research and practice. This group also realized that it was unlikely that any single individual's work would provide the breakthrough that would transform education. Without concerted collaboration among leaders in the field, second-order change in schools would not be likely to occur.

The consortium, founded in 1986, continued until 1992. Not long afterward, discussions began that led to the establishment of the Collaborative for Academic, Social, and Emotional Learning (CASEL) in 1995. CASEL expanded the focus of the consortium conceptually and programmatically. It established a term—social-emotional learning (SEL)—to reflect emerging research into the role of emotions in competence and resilience. According to the emerging SEL theory, young people equipped with skills, and the corresponding prosocial attitudes and beliefs, would be more likely to make healthy, caring, ethical, and responsible decisions, and to avoid engaging in behaviors with negative consequences such as interpersonal violence, substance abuse, and bullying (Elias et al., 1997).

SEL theory emphasized that emotions affect how and what students learn, and that young people's ability to engage in and sustain caring relationships is a necessary vehicle for deep and lasting learning (Elias et al., 1997). In a landmark book that brought together the research evidence about SEL and academic success, Zins, Weissberg, Wang, and Walberg (2004) concluded that successful academic performance by students depends on (a) students' social-emotional skills for participatory competence; (b) their approaching education with a sense of positive purpose; and (c) the presence of safe, supportive classroom and school climates that foster respectful, challenging, and engaging learning communities. It is the totality of these conditions, and the processes they imply, that are now best referred to collectively as social-emotional learning, rather than continuing to view SEL as linked primarily to a set of skills and programs that teach them.

CASEL continues as of this writing. The leadership of CASEL is largely that of the consortium group, plus a number of peers who joined later. Because CASEL's youngest members are in their mid-50s, we have been forced to confront the question of how our future leaders will emerge. CASEL has undertaken efforts to promote the next generation of leadership through increased efforts at mentoring, by providing opportunities for collaboration, and by recognizing and showcasing the accomplishments of those who appear to have the potential to be future leaders in the field.

This chapter represents an intersection of two goals: understanding important influences in the emergence of leadership at a relatively early point in the leadership trajectory, and providing an opportunity for young leaders to share their particular stories. What qualifies these individuals is that they have apprenticed with established leaders in the field of social-emotional learning in schools, and they have been recognized by their mentors and a broad collection of others, in and out of CASEL, who have evaluated their work as making substantial contributions to the field.

This chapter represents an intersection of two goals: understanding important influences in the emergence of leadership at a relatively early point in the leadership trajectory, and providing an opportunity for young leaders to share their particular stories.

Each of these four leaders—Jennifer Vargo, Paul Flaspohler, Melissa Reeves, and Victoria Blakeney—presents an analysis of his or her leadership trajectory. Each was asked to comment on formative personal and professional influences on the path to leadership, describe key individuals and concepts that proved to be helpful in shaping the leader's work and approach to leadership, and offer recommendations to aspiring leaders in school-based SEL and related fields.

An examination of themes that cut across their trajectories follows their contributions.

JENNIFER VARGO

Formative Experiences

As a young girl who grew up in a lower-middle-class Polish neighborhood in Ohio, I felt safe walking to school and playing outside with my friends, knowing that my mom and my friends' moms were at home, peering out their windows to make sure we weren't getting into mischief. I lived in a caring community where teachers, family, and friends would take time to talk, listen, and ask me questions about who I wanted to be. I was encouraged to dream big and work hard.

Fortunately for me, I loved school. School was a safe place to explore my thoughts and feelings and to challenge the status quo. My competitive side led me to compare myself academically with classmates and my older brother. Whenever I felt sad and defeated because I didn't always achieve the highest grade, my mother consistently told me how proud she was of me because I was a good, caring person, and I always tried my best to do well. I believe these qualities have served me well as I continue to develop as a person and a leader.

When I was 9 years old, my parents told us that they were divorcing. As I struggled with the divorce, living apart from my mother and watching our family slip into poverty, I learned quickly that a safe, secure environment could be lost in an instant. Given the change in economics, I found myself leaving a K–8 school with a graduating class of 10 to attend an inner-city high school with 1,200 students. The lessons learned from my mother and the skills reinforced in my Catholic education enabled me, despite my fears, to build important relationships with my new peers and teachers.

One day, before class started, my calculus teacher asked me what kind of college I was thinking of attending. I hadn't even told him that I was planning on going to college, but he had high expectations for me. I told him I was looking for a small liberal arts school in Ohio. Our school's math team was competing at Denison University, and he asked me if I'd like to ride along to look at the campus. Had it not been for that teacher taking an interest in me and my future, my life's journey could have been completely different.

Had it not been for that teacher taking an interest in me and my future, my life's journey could have been completely different.

Life as a student at Denison opened my eyes to a world that I thought was out of my reach. I met friends from families of wealth and privilege. They had explored places that I had only read about and had experiences that were beyond my reality. This transition to a new life was extremely difficult. During my freshman year, I realized that the education I had received at South High School lacked the academic rigor that my college friends had received in their high-achieving high schools. I remember studying endlessly for my zoology tests, asking for and receiving extra help from my professor, and yet still failing the tests. I discovered that many of my peers had taken advanced classes in high school. Clearly, I was not as academically prepared as my peers. If it had not been for my brother and my professors encouraging me to persevere, I believe I would have dropped out thinking that I wasn't smart enough to earn a college degree.

I was further buoyed by my two childhood passions: dance and helping children to achieve their dreams. My family could not afford to send me to actual dance classes, but during my freshman year at Denison I took a dance class as an elective. My instructor was impressed with my natural abilities and saw my love for dance. She encouraged me to take other dance classes and to audition for the dance concert even though most of the other dancers had 10 years or more of training. By my senior year, I was majoring in dance, was a student leader in the dance department, and was fulfilling my childhood dream of choreographing and dancing. Dancing did more than fulfill a childhood dream—it saved me from dropping out of college.

My experiences at Denison strengthened my desire to help children from the inner city achieve academically. While in college I was enlightened by the philosopher John Dewey, specifically his work *Democracy in Education* (1944). His belief that education should go beyond teaching facts and should build critical-thinking and problem-solving skills that students would integrate into their lives as citizens and human beings made absolute sense to me. I had *lived* this philosophy as I learned to make good decisions throughout my life. I was also influenced by the writings of Jonathan Kozol, particularly his book *Savage Inequalities* (1992). This text mirrored my own experiences and brought attention to the inequalities that perpetuate the gap between rich and poor. Having experienced this firsthand strengthened my passion and desire to help inner-city children receive a good education.

As graduation from college approached, I remember telling a friend that I'd like to fulfill another childhood dream: helping poor children in Africa. I thought it was an impossible dream, as I had never been out of Ohio. He knew me well and said, "Jen, it is absolutely possible! Research it and figure it out." Six months later I was a volunteer for a nongovernmental organization, fund-raising my way to Africa. One year after graduation, I was in Maputo, Mozambique, teaching Portuguese and math to first- and second-grade African children.

My experience in Africa changed my life. I went there full of my American idealism, determined to make their Third World education better. Armed with modern cooperative learning techniques and time management strategies, I was confident that I could positively affect students' learning. On my last day on the project, I overheard the African teachers laughing about my crazy American ways. I was hurt and angry about working hard and not being appreciated. Then, upon reflection, I was forced to laugh at myself for being ignorant and unaware that I had been working alone the entire year. As I packed to return home, one valuable lesson I took with me was that in order for change to occur, people must *want* change, and they must be a part of developing any changes. To be a leader is to help people see why change is necessary and to their benefit and to include them in the process of creating the change.

When I returned from Africa, I decided that helping children succeed in school was my life passion. For 6 months, I worked as a teacher's assistant in a Cleveland public school. I watched hours of education time pass by without children learning because the students were unable or unwilling to engage in the lessons. The school had numerous discipline problems, several students were failing, and teacher morale was extremely low. Many of the students came from poor single-parent homes, and their neighborhoods were riddled with violence and drugs. The administrators and teachers were ill-equipped to deal with the students' nonacademic challenges that were preventing them from learning. Moreover, they relied on unsuccessful discipline and behavior modification strategies to motivate students to do their work. The assistant principal asked me if I had any ideas of punishments that would make students do their work! It was clear that both staff and students needed additional skills and supports to address these issues. This experience as a teacher's assistant influenced my decision that if I were to affect children's lives, I needed to address school issues and problems from a more sociological perspective.

Thus I entered the College of Social Work to pursue a career in school social work. My initial thought was that I would help students achieve academically by doing individual counseling and linking them and their families to community services. Adelman and Taylor's (1997) work on systems of learning supports helped me to understand the need for schools to build an infrastructure that will support a comprehensive system of prevention, intervention, and linkages to community services. I learned quickly that, despite the noblest intentions, a single social worker doing individual counseling was not going to reach the majority of students who were failing their classes. There were simply too many issues, too many needs, and not enough resources. This was the beginning of a new career path for me.

> I learned quickly that, despite the noblest intentions, a single social worker doing individual counseling was not going to reach the majority of students who were failing their classes.

Influential People

In reflecting on my career path and life journey, I see many key moments and just as many influential people who have shepherded me along the way. Most influential was my mother. She raised me to be compassionate, empathetic, and grateful. I remember crying together while watching the starving children in Africa on the Save the Children fund-raising commercials, wishing there was something we could do to help. These social and emotional competencies were reinforced during my Catholic school education, which provided me with opportunities to reflect and to make good choices. It was during my nightly prayers, reflecting on my actions for the day, that I would learn the most about myself and others. I was fortunate to have caring family and friends with whom to share and process these reflections, which always led me in the direction of learning ways to do things better. The process of reflection with others has been instrumental in helping me to understand and discover who I am and to determine my purpose in life.

When I took a position as a program specialist for mental health and education initiatives at the Center for Learning Excellence at Ohio State University, I was privileged to work with Dr. Mary Lou Rush and Dr. Joseph E. Zins in developing a grant that would help schools build a comprehensive system of learning supports. This work integrated all of our passions and expertise: Dr. Rush's expertise in policy, Dr. Zins' passion for SEL, and my knowledge of linking schools to community services. Mary Lou served as my mentor, schooling me in education policy, politics, and child development.

Joe Zins and I spoke extensively about SEL, and he taught me that it is our duty as educators to develop children into compassionate leaders. His passion inspired me to learn more about SEL. As I read *Promoting Social and Emotional Learning: Guidelines for Educators* (coauthored by Joe; Elias et al., 1997), I realized that I had learned SEL skills in my Catholic grade school and from my mother—skills that I have used throughout my life.

During that time, Joe died suddenly. Although I had known him for only 5 months, he had a profound impact on my life. I still reflect on how fortunate I am to be living my dream: learning and growing in a safe and supportive environment doing work that is essential for all children. I believe my work is helping the children in Ohio to attain their own dreams through the portal of education. That doorway of education should lead to developing SEL competencies of reflection, compassion, and empathy. Joe reminded me that teaching children these skills is the "right thing to do." Through his example, I learned that to be a leader in SEL is to guide, coach, and model, and that educators and students create change through the process of reflection and problem solving. I know that SEL skills combined with support and encouragement from my family, teachers, and adult mentors have helped me develop into the leader that I am today.

Since Joe's passing, I continue to carry on his work in my position as a leader in the Ohio Department of Education. I serve as Family and Community Engagement Coordinator in the Center for Students, Families, and Communities, where I manage the Office of Family and Community Engagement Initiatives. Recent initiatives include developing the newly adopted State Board of Education Parent and Family Involvement policy, creating and disseminating parent education workshops, and building the capacity of districts and schools to create and implement effective family and community engagement strategies.

Recommendations for Aspiring Leaders

1. Work directly in schools, either through academic field placements or volunteering, observing student and teacher relationships and interactions. Talk with teachers, administrators, and students about challenges they face in school and engage them in problem-solving the challenges. This will ground you in the everyday realities of individuals whom you ultimately will lead and with whom you will collaborate.

2. Find mentors with field experience to help guide your work.

3. Start with the "low-hanging fruit" and celebrate all successes. In the beginning, implement strategies that are easy to accomplish. Celebrate the successes and build momentum for implementing the next phase of strategies.

Start with the "low-hanging fruit" and celebrate all successes.

Paul Flaspohler

Formative Experiences

I decided to pursue an advanced degree in psychology 6 months after returning from serving as a Peace Corps volunteer in West Africa. I am now an assistant professor in the Department of Psychology at

Miami University. My pathway to this position was not typical, but my experiences and training have shaped my approach to working with children, families, and schools. The lessons I have drawn from this work may be useful for those planning and supporting the development of others who are interested in the important work of facilitating children's development and in social and emotional learning. Fate and choice provided me with experiences, exposure to ideas, and opportunities to work with great people who have been kind enough to share their expertise. As a result, I have learned to learn from others and, in turn, have used that strategy to promote the success of the clients, school systems, and students with whom I work.

My own experience of public education was instrumental in developing my world view and shaped my commitment to improving public schools. I attended a large urban elementary school in the early 1970s. Most of my classmates were African American; many lived in public housing. The school's experimental curriculum included open classrooms and Individually Guided Education. My teachers were young, inspired, and politically active (I walked picket lines with my first-grade teacher). Today, many of my elementary school classmates are successful professionals—among them doctors, lawyers, teachers, and politicians. By the time I graduated from college, however, several of my classmates from elementary school were dead from drugs or gang- or family-related violence. The high school I attended was a large public college-preparatory school attended by many of the brightest students in Cincinnati, Ohio. The student body was diverse with respect to race, religion, and economic status. My personal norms and expectations about education and culture grew out of these early experiences. In short, I came to believe that diversity in education was a common experience; it was the only experience I knew.

At Xavier University in Cincinnati, I was an underachieving undergraduate, but was fortunate to receive a high-quality education. Xavier presented several opportunities to experience cultural differences firsthand. First, Xavier's campus was significantly different from my elementary and secondary schools in that most of the students at Xavier were (like me) white, middle class, and raised Catholic. Unlike me, however, most of my fellow Xavier students had been educated in predominantly white, Catholic institutions. Xavier also provided opportunities to study abroad at the University of Vienna, where I forged enduring friendships with students from around the world.

In both of these early experiences, I was challenged by the limitations of my own life experiences. At Xavier, I was challenged to reconcile my unusual early educational experience (which I had always assumed was typical) and subsequent emerging worldview with the different worldviews of college peers who were ostensibly culturally similar to me. In Vienna, I was challenged to reconcile my Western ideology against the experiences and ideas of faculty and students from around the world, including countries that Ronald Reagan referred to as "the Evil Empire."

My time in the Peace Corps built a further appreciation for the power of experience, place, and culture. I spent nearly 3 years living in West Africa fully immersed in a culture far different from my own. Through both the Peace Corps and European experiences, I learned firsthand about the power of place and culture, coming to understand how my own early experience created "truths" and expectations that proved less true when examined through the lens of another culture.

My time in the Peace Corps built a further appreciation for the power of experience, place, and culture.

Living in West Africa also gave me the ability to exercise patience in unfamiliar situations, which served me well upon my return, as it took me 10 years to earn my PhD. I enrolled in undergraduate psychology courses at the University of Cincinnati (UC) and pursued experiences in both research and practice. I "swept the laboratory" for Robert Frank at UC and for Kathy Hart at Xavier while I gained basic research skills. I worked in in-patient psychiatry as a mental health technician, gaining appreciation for the complexity of being a member of interdisciplinary treatment teams working with adults and children. These experiences helped me develop a "two hat" approach to research and practice: training in psychology seems to support acting as a scientist in one set of contexts and a practitioner in another. I was compelled to confront my two-hat approach during the course of completing my PhD, as described further below.

Influential People

I received my PhD from the University of South Carolina (USC). At USC, I received training in clinical and community psychology. The clinical training model at USC afforded the opportunity to serve clients with supervision from varying theoretical orientations, from behavioral to psychodynamic to humanistic. Ongoing treatment with long-term clients was usually overseen by a series of different supervisors, which forced me to navigate the theoretical orientation of each one. I had challenging and compelling supervision from the late Mervyn Wagner and from Herman Salzburg, Diane Follingstad, Will Drennen, and Pauline Pagliocca. Seeing the same client through the lenses of different supervisors (and differing theoretical orientations) compels one to make sense of the work beyond one's own particular view of change. Shifting paradigms in supervision provided me with opportunities to experience and explore consistency and difference across therapeutic modalities.

At USC, we were also exposed to the principles and values of community psychology. In a way, we were learning to participate in the mental health service delivery system while also learning to criticize the purpose, intentions, and structures of that system. We read George Albee's views about the futility of psychotherapy while gaining skills in individual, group, and family therapy, again creating an opportunity and incentive to reconcile divergent perspectives. I received outstanding training and practical experience in community psychology from Jean Ann Linney and, in particular, from Abe Wandersman. Thanks to Jean Ann Linney, I spent 48 hours as an inpatient in a state psychiatric hospital (through a program called Step Into My Shoes)—a significant experiential learning moment that fostered a deep appreciation for the experience of consumers of mental health services and the gravity of the role of mental health service provider.

My research efforts at USC also provided juxtaposing experiences. In my first 3 years there, I worked on a large prevention project with my research mentor and dissertation chair, Ron Prinz. The project, EARLY ALLIANCE (Prinz, Dumas, Smith, & Laughlin, 2000), was designed to prevent conduct disorders. I oversaw implementation of an after-school reading program that paired high school student mentors with at-risk children. Some schools absorbed the program better than others; some teachers were more willing and able to participate than others. Through EARLY ALLIANCE, I had to learn to collaborate at multiple levels: with school administrators, teachers, undergraduate volunteers, high school mentors, and the children themselves. EARLY ALLIANCE was as brilliantly designed as it was challenging to implement, providing firsthand exposure to the gap between research and practice.

My "two hat" approach to psychology continued for several years at USC. A conversation with Abe Wandersman about evaluation and accountability opened the door for reconciling the gap in my own pursuit of research and practice. I had naively believed that "in the real world" practitioners regularly engaged in evaluation of services. After all, training in a scientist-practitioner model should provide both the skills and the motivation to plan, implement, evaluate, and improve services. The realities of evaluation gave rise to many of my subsequent research and practice efforts, affording the opportunity to align the two hats of research and practice. I worked closely with Abe on applied and conceptual projects, including the development of an accountability system for South Carolina's First Steps to School Readiness Initiative (Flaspohler et al., 2003) and on the development of principles of Empowerment Evaluation (Wandersman et al., 2004). Abe teaches through juxtaposing the theoretical and the practical, including practical engagement with communities and community problems in courses on environmental psychology and program evaluation. Through these projects and his courses, I came to admire and appreciate his uncanny ability to motivate students and support the development of projects. Abe would pull together the right set of people, provide a compelling task, delineate "the process," and let the work develop.

The opportunities to reconcile the juxtaposition of clinical training and community work, of the didactic and the practical, of research and practice shaped my thinking and have been critical to my current efforts in research and action. Training as a clinician, I believe, makes me more facile in assisting with the promotion of change at every level. It helps to be able to conceptualize individual change processes in the movement toward supporting organizational changes and to predict and prepare for the impact of organizational changes on individuals within an organization.

As a new professor at Miami University, I was introduced to a community of practice dedicated to the promotion of mental health in schools. This interdisciplinary group has welcomed me and provided opportunities to develop and redefine the goals and purposes of my research. Among my many colleagues in this realm are the late Joe Zins, as well as Dawn Anderson-Butcher, Mark Weist, Steve Evans,

Julie Owens, Robert Burke, Hal Lawson, Seth Bernstein, Karen Weston, and many others. None of this would have happened without the support and encouragement of Carl Paternite, with whom I have worked closely at Miami.

Recommendations for Aspiring Leaders

1. My students are teaching me about how best to support their development as competent, practicing psychologists (with one integrated hat). I've been blessed to have been able to recruit and work with several exceptional students, and I hope I'm learning how to create some abilities that leaders truly need: setting a compelling task, identifying the right people to do a job, delineating the process clearly, and letting the work develop.

2. One cannot prescribe specific experiences, and one should not expect that the same experiences will produce the same outcome or pathway for different individuals. But one can prescribe the pursuit of new and challenging experiences that are likely to compel one to understand and work beyond the limitations of one's experience. Students interested in pursuing a profession dedicated to the promotion of social and emotional health and well-being should seek applied experiences that mirror, complement, or challenge the didactic experience of higher education. I recommend strongly the experience of working with people in different disciplines and with different theories, approached with a willingness to examine the limitations of one's own thinking and the value of others.

3. Seek out opportunities for cultural immersion. To be successful as an agent of change working with schools, one should be aware of one's own cultural blinders and limitations. I have watched many fail because they do not recognize or understand the unique cultures of schools and how cultural influences change. Immersion in another culture provides the opportunity for

To be successful as an agent of change working with schools, one should be aware of one's own cultural blinders and limitations. I have watched many fail because they do not recognize or understand the unique cultures of schools and how cultural influences change.

self-exploration of values and norms and fosters appreciation of norms and values in other cultures. Once one has had such experiences, every subsequent engagement with schools and communities becomes an experience of culture wherein one is compelled to learn about and participate in the culture of the new school or community.

MELISSA A. REEVES

Formative Experiences

When I look back, it becomes clear to me that my leadership capacity for SEL really began in second grade. I vividly remember, as a first grader, sitting in reading group next to the teacher. We were practicing sounding out words and it was my turn. I began to sound out the word and heard my teacher's stern voice. I don't remember specifically what she said, but I do remember that I didn't get it right and that she was angry with me.

At that point, the little first-grade girl who loved to learn shut down—not only in class but with reading at home. My mom tried coaxing me to read, yet I remained silent. Somehow my mom convinced me to talk about what had happened in class. From a 6-year-old perspective I had failed and was not good at reading. After my mother spoke with the principal, I was assigned to the best second-grade teacher in the school, Ms. Bean. Ms. Bean believed in me, reinstilled my love for learning and reading, and told me I could do anything. She was patient in helping me overcome my fears and encouraged me when I was hesitant. I firmly believe that I would not have received a college degree, let alone a doctorate, if it were not for Ms. Bean. Once I learned how to read and gained in confidence, you could not get me to put a book down—and that's still true today! All I wanted for Christmas were Nancy Drew books; to this day I have the entire hardbound collection, which I refuse to part with. To me those books are more than just books; they symbolize how much I overcame with the support and encouragement of a teacher.

I never forgot that experience of being helped, and of how it saved me. As a senior in high school, wanting to help others, I volunteered each day as a peer assistant in a multi-categorical special needs classroom. Though I was not aware of it at the time, this experience was more than just helping the teacher and students with schoolwork; it was helping my own peers with disabilities develop friendships and feel part of their own peer group. This experience led me to double major in psychology and special education with an emphasis in behavioral disorders, which then led to my earning a special education teaching license. My classroom experiences helped me realize that I needed to better understand the emotional aspect of why these students were exhibiting emotional and behavioral struggles. This led me to an M.A. in Counseling Psychology and a Ph.D. in School Psychology, which opened my eyes to realizing how much the environment, resiliency factors, and internal and external support systems all interact to help students succeed. (So many times I observed firsthand how these variables can interact to frustrate students.) Through these experiences my passion for initiating change at the "systems level" and effecting change by looking through the lens of school climate and peer influence came to fruition.

> *My classroom experiences helped me realize that I needed to better understand the emotional aspect of why these students were exhibiting emotional and behavioral struggles.*

I was fortunate to work in the Cherry Creek School District, a supportive and innovative district in a suburb of Denver, where educating the "whole child" was valued. My first years were anything but easy, however. The elementary school where I worked was fragmented in every way. The academic curriculum was chosen by individual teachers or grade-level teams, with minimal collaboration with other grade levels. This led to inconsistency in regard to grade-level expectations and cooperation among the teachers. The staff had developed their own cliques, with select teachers having a powerful influence in the school. In regard to student dynamics, there was not a well-established culture promoting SEL. In addition, the new principal was the fifth one in the past 7 years. The teaching staff was fatigued, burnt out, and overwhelmed with the emotional issues that students were bringing to the classroom, as well as by the curricular demands.

The principal and I noticed these dynamics and realized that we needed to foster leadership and build a sense of community, with both the staff and the student body. I was fortunate that the principal, Denise Maxwell, was a former teacher of both special education and general education who understood students' widely varying learning and emotional needs. Essentially, what the school really needed at all levels was SEL—recognizing and managing emotions, caring about and respecting others, developing positive relationships, making good decisions, and behaving responsibly and ethically.

Ironically, some teachers did not want change and overtly resisted our initial efforts; therefore, we began working collaboratively with both individuals and small groups of teachers who were open to new ideas. We implemented teacher training, recognition programs, and activities that recognized "caring deeds" and helping others. A fifth-grade teacher and I also wrote three different grants that facilitated a multiyear training program titled Building Assets for Bright Futures. This program allowed us to train teachers and support staff in a family and organizational systems perspective, which gave them a better understanding of how family, school, and community experiences interact to influence the perspectives we have, the decisions we make, and the ways in which we behave and respond to situations. This same program also taught intervention strategies, classroom management, and communication skills. These teachers, in turn, served on our "Care Team" (problem-solving/student assistance team) to help other teachers develop positive intervention strategies focused on meeting the social-emotional needs of students.

In 2 years, we saw a 50 percent decrease in behavioral office referrals and an increase in teacher confidence and ability to meet student needs. This training allowed teachers to better understand their own teaching dynamics and the dynamics of classroom interactions, while also focusing on increasing their interpersonal skills with students and parents to establish a positive classroom management system.

For students, the school social worker and I taught a school-wide bully-proofing and assets-building curriculum. We developed and sustained a caring community in countless ways, such as the following:

- We implemented student and staff recognition programs for caring deeds, whereby students and *all* staff (including parent volunteers, custodial staff, and food service personnel) nominated each other for a monthly recognition assembly, and photos of honorees were placed on a recognition bulletin board.
- We created a Garden of Kindness where students were able to take turns building and cultivating a garden on school

grounds. Symbolically speaking, they were learning to care for each other, even when natural nurturing (e.g., rain for the garden, parental support for the child) was lacking and more TLC was needed.

- We started the first-ever student-anchored morning news announcements highlighting school news and positive deeds.
- We initiated schoolwide involvement in the Broncos Food Drive to make donations to a local food pantry, and raised money for a student who was diagnosed with cancer.
- A variety of support groups and individual interventions were also offered, including grief and loss, anger management, social skills, and anxiety management.

Our goal throughout all of these innovations was to help students learn and reflect on their own emotions and decision making, developing an awareness of how their behaviors affect others and building self-esteem and positive connections with adults and school activities. To support the school's parents, we held parent seminars regarding a variety of issues and worked with our family liaison to offer a bilingual parent group to help our Spanish-speaking parents feel more connected to the school. It was so exciting to see ideas turn into reality—all beginning with positive leadership and vision!

> *Our goal throughout all of these innovations was to help students learn and reflect on their own emotions and decision making, developing an awareness of how their behaviors affect others and building self-esteem and positive connections with adults and school activities.*

After 5 years at this school (and, I must say, largely because my leadership at the building level was showcased to district administrators), I became the district's Social-Emotional Behavior Specialist to help coordinate programs for students with a variety of social and emotional challenges. Many of the students in these programs had not been successful in school, did not see school as a positive experience, and often did not believe in themselves or feel that others believed in them. All of these students had the ability to be successful, and many had strengths that had been overlooked. I considered my new position to be essential in helping students, teachers, and parents to acknowledge students' strengths, to make positive connections with school, and to build on the assets of both students and teachers to foster the core components of SEL.

By using positive behavior supports, direct instruction in life skills (e.g., anger management strategies), and focusing on building assets, we were able to begin making the systems change from a deficit model to a strength-based model.

As I write about all that I have done, I must emphasize that I could not have done any of this without the support of many others. I have always believed that if you model collaborative leadership, listen, and provide the necessary resources (including emotional support), then you will see great things happen for teachers and students.

In addition, many of our schools did not directly discuss social-emotional interventions and were not held directly accountable for designing and implementing social-emotional goals for students. This led to many discussions of the "gaps" in not only academic programming, but also in social-emotional learning. I facilitated discussions with administrators, the staff development office, and coordinators on how to fill those gaps, and we began developing a multitiered service delivery model for both academics and behavior. Finally, in everything we did, we integrated equity and excellence by addressing the cultural needs and the achievement gap, and by being aware of how diversity affects what we do.

Influential People

In addition to Ms. Bean, Dr. Patty Meek was one of my first mentors while I completed a practicum in school psychology. She had the highest of ethics and believed all kids can learn, and she truly lived this motto. She never gave up until every child was learning. As a school psychologist, she became trained in a specialized reading curriculum that motivated her to return to school to earn her teaching license so as to teach these skills. I observed her teaching middle school students to read who had never read beyond a first-grade level. It took time and persistence, but the joy and smiles on their faces when they read a "real" book for the first time is something I'll never forget. Dr. Meek worked tirelessly for those students and truly made a difference; they left her room feeling confident and self-assured in ways they had never felt before. Although I had many other mentors who saw my potential and fostered my leadership abilities, Dr. Meek lived SEL for her students—and this is what being an educator is about!

I have also been influenced by the work of two authors in particular. Robert Brooks, who wrote *The Self-Esteem Teacher: Seeds of Self-Esteem* (1991), introduced me to the concept of an "island of competence." So often we tend to work out of a "deficit model"—what students can't do—instead of using a "strength-based" model—what they *can* do. This was so true for the students I worked with. Positive reinforcement and feeling success was not something these children had much experience with, and the notion of building on their strengths touched me deeply. This was also a concept that teachers could understand and embrace, without feeling overwhelmed by having to implement a specific behavioral intervention plan for each student. This approach is all about encouragement and accepting students for where they are and who they are, while helping them reach their full potential and experience success.

Beverly Daniel Tatum's powerful book, *Why Are All the Black Kids Sitting in the Cafeteria? A Psychologist Explains the Development of Racial Identity* (2003), forced me to reflect on my own prejudices. It also gave me insight into the dynamics between the various students and groups I was seeing at school, and how others may perceive my actions (or inactions) in ways that are different from what I would expect. The entire staff of our school read this book; it led to many intense discussions about how our own personal history, experiences, prejudices (even those we were not aware of), and interactions affect each other and our school climate.

Recommendations for Aspiring Leaders

1. Always do what is best for the student. Whenever tough decisions are needed, this is the number-one rule that should guide every decision. Below is a quote by the child psychologist Haim Ginott that I use in every university course I teach to educators:

> *Always do what is best for the student. Whenever tough decisions are needed, this is the number-one rule that should guide every decision.*

I've come to the frightening conclusion that I am the decisive element in the classroom. My personal approach creates the climate. My daily mood makes the weather. As a teacher, I possess a tremendous power to make a child's life miserable or joyous. I can be a tool of torture or an instrument of healing; I can humiliate or humor, hurt or heal. In all situations, it is my response that decides whether a crisis will be escalated or deescalated and a child humanized or dehumanized.

2. Never underestimate the difference one individual can make; however, if you can surround yourself with positively focused mentors and colleagues who model SEL, you can make an even larger difference. As a personal example of this, in addition to my work in my own district, I've been involved in state- and national-level leadership by serving on my state's board (Colorado Society of School Psychologists) as well as a national organization executive council (National Association of School Psychologists). These positions have allowed me to see the world beyond my school district. I helped to bring professional development workshops specifically focused on social-emotional development, have testified in front of legislative committees, made "hill visits" in Washington, D.C., to promote school mental health issues, and have helped to develop policies and practices advocating for the expansion of mental health services for children in schools. I strongly recommend that all educators become involved in leadership roles. Whether at the local, state, or national level, these roles help to develop a larger perspective, a better understanding of the field and resources available, and a network of colleagues to help you become a better professional.

3. Give yourself permission to not have all the answers. Ask for help, and be open to new ideas. Fostering relationships, building connections, listening to strengths and needs, respecting various viewpoints, always doing what is best for kids, and caring about the individual person are the core beliefs that underlie everything I have done and that have shaped my professional career.

VICTORIA BLAKENEY

Formative Experiences

I was a high school English teacher before I became involved in SEL. As a teacher, two of my classes in particular prompted my interest in this field. First, I taught a course called Teen Issues Literature. Rather than teaching the traditional canon, I learned how to teach about such issues as drug and alcohol prevention, decision making, goal setting, teen violence, and relationships.

I grew so interested in the subject matter that I asked my principal for a chance to use what I was learning to help the whole school. At that time, we didn't have anything systematic in place to help prevent harassment and bullying. So I began working with my colleagues to research, design, and implement an alternative to suspension classes for students who were given disciplinary referrals for bullying a classmate.

At about this same time, I decided to attend the University of Alaska, Anchorage (UAA) to earn a master's degree in Educational Leadership. While implementing the harassment program, I had discovered in myself a real enjoyment both in the synergy of working with my colleagues and in watching the amazing successes that grew out of teaching skills in self-awareness and self-management to the students in the anti-harassment classes. I wanted to learn how to do more of both of those things. I wanted to show teachers and schools how to implement Social and Emotional Learning programs. I just didn't know those terms yet.

While taking my UAA classes, I continued to teach and was asked to team teach a special tenth-grade English class of students identified as "not likely to pass the high school graduation qualifying exam." In one of my UAA classes, I'd been learning techniques in community building in a classroom. My team teacher and I decided to employ these activities in this classroom—and our traditionally disconnected students began thinking of themselves as a part of a group. The payoff in academics was huge. That spring, when our students had their first chance to take the high school graduation qualifying exam, we had a 93 percent success rate! (The school average was only 68 percent.) The kids "not likely to pass" blew the average out of the water, and I became a believer!

Another master class, Innovations in Education, taught one key concept that stood out to me: An innovation has to be owned by everyone. An innovation has to begin with a champion, but it cannot remain dependent on that champion if it is to truly result in school reform. I saw that very problem in my own school district. Our district was one of the first to adopt the Resolving Conflicts Creatively Program (RCCP), yet the program was still being implemented in pockets that depended on the

An innovation has to begin with a champion, but it cannot remain dependent on that champion if it is to truly result in school reform.

building champion, rather than becoming a part of the school district's culture.

Our district superintendent, Carol Comeau, called together a team of forward-thinking individuals—including Michael Kerosky, supervisor of Safe and Drug-Free Schools, and Dr. Enid Silverstein, executive director of Curriculum and Instruction—and asked for suggestions on how to combat this problem. The team did some research. Michael discovered the Collaborative for Academic, Social, and Emotional Learning (CASEL) and their work with the Illinois SEL standards. Enid, who was in the process of implementing a 6-year comprehensive plan for the district, recommended that we incorporate SEL as a curriculum and include it in the strategic 6-year plan that had been approved by the school board. These two moves formed the foundation for hiring an SEL curriculum coordinator.

I had been planning to leave Alaska. I was in the final year of my master's program, and my husband and I planned to move closer to our families at the end of the school year. When the job posting was e-mailed to me, I was so sure we were leaving that I didn't even plan to open it. But then I thought, "Well, I could at least see what it says." When I read the description, it finally gave me the term for the work I had been trying to do all along: *social and emotional learning.* Now, 4 years later, we're still living in Alaska, and we plan to be here indefinitely. I have a dream job.

Influential People

I began working as the SEL curriculum coordinator in October 2004, but really knew nothing about SEL except what I had picked up experientially along the way. Therefore, one of my first tasks was to learn as much as I could about the field itself. I read both *Building Academic Success on Social and Emotional Learning* (Zins et al., 2004) and *Promoting Social and Emotional Learning* (Elias et al., 1997), and I contacted CASEL almost immediately to ask them about the process they had used to develop the Illinois standards. At the same time, I needed to create a committee of community and school personnel who could help to write the Anchorage School District's Social and Emotional Learning Standards before I could begin any real work.

Incredibly, two amazing leaders in the field of SEL visited Anchorage at about this time. Linda Lantieri has been coming to

Alaska for almost 20 years—first to help with the implementation of RCCP, and later to speak to our teachers on ways in which they can build inner resiliency and self-confidence in their students. When I heard her speak, I knew I'd found my role model. Linda builds SEL for kids by taking care of the teachers' needs. As she helps staff nurture their own social and emotional skills, they become better prepared to help their students learn them. This was a key piece of learning for me. Teaching SEL is a habit of practice for the teacher.

Next, Janet Patti came to train our principals on her book with James Tobin, *Smart School Leaders: Leading With Emotional Intelligence* (2006). Her training came at the perfect time; she was able to explain the work with such clarity that my understanding of SEL solidified. Her approach to SEL is one of systematic skill building. I took that understanding to the first of our steering committee meetings, and it galvanized our team as we began writing our standards. However, we still couldn't conceptualize how the implementation of these standards would look until Mary Utne O'Brien of CASEL invited us to Chicago for a training on their *Sustainable Schoolwide Social and Emotional Learning Implementation Guide and Toolkit.* The CASEL rubrics and other tools gave us a conceptual framework for what we were trying to do.

Finally, even though I could now conceptualize implementation, I couldn't picture what that would mean for a person in the classroom. Two things happened at the same time to help me. First, a focus group with students showed me that they didn't want just to be taught the SEL skills in a vacuum; they wanted relevance and a chance to practice those skills. To that end, I began working with an expert in experiential education to teach me how to facilitate initiatives that would allow students to practice SEL in group problem-solving situations. In addition, I began studying culturally responsive teaching practices. It became obvious that culturally responsive practices and SEL go hand-in-hand. Both our climate and our practitioners must be culturally responsive in order for our students to reach their full potential, both academically and in their social-emotional skills.

As we began our implementation, I realized a couple of important things. First, SEL in our district is not, and cannot be, dependent on my being there. Our district owns SEL, and we have borrowed heavily from experts in the field. We have buy-in from our community and our teachers because so many of us see ourselves in the work that is being done, because so many have contributed to the work, and because we have used the most current research available to guide our work. I do everything as a part of a team—a school team, the Safe and Drug-Free Schools team, the curriculum department, the culturally responsive education committee, or an ad hoc committee, depending on the circumstance. It's the folks in the field who are really going to make the difference, so I need to be sure I'm hearing from them when we work on our projects.

Second, we never hesitate to celebrate our successes. Often we are so very busy working on the minutiae that it helps to stop occasionally and look back at where we started and enjoy the distance we've traveled. Such celebrations also keep people inspired to continue on the journey, as we have a long way to go before we can say we have reached the end.

Recommendations for Aspiring Leaders

1. Listen. Listen to parents, colleagues, administrators, and especially to students. We use our social and emotional skills all day, every day. As a result, people everywhere have the potential to be experts in building SEL. Listen to them, honor them, and use their collective wisdom to help move your mission forward.

2. Understand the political climate within which you work. Learn to walk through open doors when they are offered. They might not lead in exactly the direction you were originally planning to go, but you'll learn to accept them as the direction in which the climate is right for moving ahead. Implementation is a long-term endeavor, so you can't be in a hurry to force open doors that are not ready to open yet. Do pilot projects in small pockets, and wait until those pilot projects are noticed and the next door opens to you and your work.

3. Back up everything with data. Stay current with research, whether brain research, best-practices research, culturally responsive research, or some other. Study the data your schools are providing. We use the American Institute for Research's School Climate and Connectedness Survey to

gather data on students' perceptions of our schools. This survey rates the strengths and weaknesses in the culture of the schools, as well as provides data on how strong the students say their own SEL skills are. We also use student focus groups and allow the information we glean from such groups to guide our process. From there, we trust that what we are doing is good for kids, and we enjoy watching growth when we find it. This is truly collaborative leadership.

REFLECTION ON THE TRAJECTORIES

According to Patti and Tobin (2006), leaders have certain essential characteristics that appear to be present early in their lives and that contribute to their growth and preparation for their moment, their opportunity for leadership. These include

- Being an avid and continuous learner;
- Having self-awareness;
- Being optimistic;
- Having effective communication skills and being a good listener;
- Possessing strong empathy;
- Being a self-directed learner;
- Having experience with facilitative-collaborative (versus authoritarian) leadership;
- Developing a strong personal and prosocial value system.

Patti and Tobin (2006) also discuss the essential benefits that are provided as a result of coaching and mentoring. The accounts of our four future leaders support their insights. Early in the lives of these four leaders, they were imbued with a sense of resilience and a bedrock of support that allowed them to weather difficulties and overcome obstacles. These attributes were strengthened and deepened by mentoring relationships to which our leaders had access. It is noteworthy that in each case, the mentoring they received was both conceptual and pragmatic. This combination also appears to be an essential feature of effective SEL leadership in schools. Moreover, seeking challenging and boundary-expanding experiences is another strong, common theme. As our focus here is on school-based SEL leadership, it is worth noting that each individual's value system is imbued with a strong sense of altruism and social justice. We believe that this will be a common denominator in enduring, effective SEL leadership.

One interesting point about examining leadership trajectories fairly early in the journey is that those factors that bring people to leadership initially do not always allow them to sustain that leadership role. Marzano, Waters, and McNulty (2005), in a meta-analysis of leadership studies, find that leaders who have a deeper impact on their organizations, and who thereby can be said to engage in second-order change, appear to embody certain dimensions that are clearly a combination of both learned and lived elements. The seven dimensions they identify and the implications for leadership behavior follow:

1. Knowledge of curriculum, instruction, and assessment. Leaders must know how an innovation will affect curriculum, instruction, and assessment practices and provide conceptual guidance in these areas.

2. Being an optimizer. Be the driving force for improvement and an advocate for the belief that exceptional results can be realized if staff members are willing to apply themselves.

3. Intellectual stimulation. Know the research and theory relating to the innovation, and foster knowledge in staff via readings and discussion.

4. Being a change agent. Be willing to challenge the status quo without guaranteeing success or insisting on the path.

5. Monitoring/evaluating. Approach formative and summative evaluation in a continuous way—for improvement and not blame.

6. Flexibility. Be directive or nondirective about the innovation as the situation warrants.

7. Ideals/beliefs. Operate in a manner that is consonant with ideals and beliefs about an innovation. As Gandhi said, "Be the change you want to see in the world."

The preceding accounts of leadership trajectories seem to confirm that all four educators embody most of these dimensions. Moreover, all are still at points in their careers where they can benefit from the forward guidance that these dimensions provide. Several related areas where relatively new leaders sometimes become hesitant include being a change agent; being the visible, optimistic driving force for change; and living one's beliefs strongly. Sometimes this happens because of a natural tendency to defer to established leaders. But as those who chronicle educational change (or the lack thereof) have noted (Kozol, 2005), our children cannot wait any longer for adults to do what is necessary to provide them with their developmental rights. That is one reason why the skills of emotionally intelligent leaders in taking action, even when the path ahead is not clear, are being given increasing emphasis in organizational circles (Goleman, 2006).

— ❧ —

The skills of emotionally intelligent leaders in taking action, even when the path ahead is not clear, are being given increasing emphasis in organizational circles.

Indeed, leaders must have courage, because *innovation means disruption*—of culture, communication, order, and patterns of participation. These elements must change if the system is to change, but during the change process there may be some who feel adversely affected, even threatened. Part of developing leadership involves being mentored through the resistance/disruptive stage of change (Patti & Tobin, 2006). Another part involves working within a forward-looking, optimistic context of collective efficacy (Sergiovanni, 2004) and cohesive and purposeful learning communities (DuFour, 1998). In practical terms, this means exposure, in team contexts, to addressing questions that are significant; having a high-quality work standard and being concerned about continuous improvement; having a sense of mutual responsibility, accountability, and interdependence; and operating with integrity and ethics—that is, with justice, compassion, tolerance, fairness, insight, and openness in decision making.

Both the consortium alluded to at the beginning of this chapter and CASEL proceeded in their development by building support structures and professional learning communities among people in multiple institutions. Very often, a critical mass of knowledgeable support does not exist within emerging leaders' home settings. While local allies and adherents should be nurtured and encouraged, simultaneous efforts must be made to reach out to those in similar situations in outside settings, as well as to ongoing sources of greater expertise (Novick, Kress, & Elias, 2002).

Finally, emerging leaders in school-based SEL—and indeed in education more generally—must have a constant agenda for ongoing learning. Being a self-directed learner, as mentioned earlier, is important, but Ten Eyck, Doolan, Cram, Scannella, and Firestone (2006) believe that best practice requires a process that is explicit and ongoing, such as a rolling action plan. They believe that there are two intersecting dimensions to consider: personal learning and organizational learning. The former involves an ongoing process of having learning goals about which one engages in ongoing contemplation and reflection, collaborative processes for building knowledge and skills, and putting learning into action. The latter moves the same process to an organizational level. This includes creating a shared vision of professional learning; maintaining a school culture that fosters professional learning and its translation to student outcomes; providing a safe and caring environment; inviting family and community collaboration into the process of vision and learning; and revisiting the process in light of ongoing local, state, national, and international developments.

Each of our four educators in this chapter has been engaged in ongoing learning around SEL, integrating SEL with other intellectual interests and traditions, and building communities in which this learning can be shared and deepened. Jennifer Vargo does this at the Ohio Department of Education; Paul Flaspohler does this through his interdisciplinary practice group at Miami University; Melissa Reeves has done this not only in her school, but increasingly through the National Association of School Psychologists; and Victoria Blakeney is building networks within the Anchorage School District and also nationally, through collaboration with her mentor, Linda Lantieri, and with CASEL.

Future research in emerging leadership should pay stronger attention to formative early life experiences than has heretofore been the norm. There is little doubt that the stories presented in this chapter suggest that strong reservoirs of emotional intelligence/SEL skills, resilience, and positive prosocial character messages were present in these individuals prior to their school leadership opportunities. The way in which competence, predilection, and opportunity converge is an important dimension in building leadership capacity, especially in an intentional way. As fields such as school-based SEL mature, attending to the process of leadership succession becomes essential. This is no less true for other innovative school change efforts. These deliberations can derive some guidance from increasing accounts of early and mid-trajectory leadership experiences, as well as tracking these trajectories over time.

REFERENCES

Adelman, H. S., & Taylor, L. (1997). System reform to address barriers to learning: Beyond school-linked services and full service schools. *American Journal of Orthopsychiatry, 67*(3), 408–421.

Brooks, R. (1991). *The self-esteem teacher: Seeds of self-esteem.* Circle Pines, MN: American Guidance Service.

Dewey, J. (1944). *Democracy in education.* New York: MacMillan.

DuFour, R. (1998). *Professional learning communities at work.* Alexandria, VA: Association for Supervision and Curriculum Development.

Elias, M. J., Weissberg, R., Zins, J., Kendall, P., Dodge, K., Jason, L., et al. (1996). Transdisciplinary collaboration among school researchers: The Consortium on the School-Based Promotion of Social Competence. *Journal of Educational and Psychological Consultation, 8,* 25–44.

Elias, M. J., Zins, J. E., Weissberg, R. P., Frey, K. S., Greenberg, M. T., Haynes, N. M., et al. (1997). *Promoting social and emotional learning guidelines for educators.* Alexandria, VA: Association for Supervision and Curriculum Development.

Flaspohler, P., Wandersman, A., Keener, D., Maxwell, K. N., Ace, A., Andrews, A., et al. (2003). Promoting program success and fulfilling accountability requirements in a statewide community-based initiative: Challenges, progress, and lessons learned. *Journal of Prevention & Intervention in the Community, 26*(2), 37–52.

Goleman, D. (2006). What makes a leader? In J. Patti & J. Tobin (Eds.), *Smart school leaders: Leading with emotional intelligence* (2nd ed.). Dubuque, IA: Kendall Hunt.

Kozol, J. (1992). *Savage inequalities: Children in America's schools.* London: Harper Perennial.

Kozol, J. (2005). Apartheid in America? *Phi Delta Kappan, 87*(4), 264–275.

Marzano, R. J., Waters, T., & McNulty, B. (2005). *School leadership that works: From research to results.* Alexandria, VA: Association for Supervision and Curriculum Development.

Novick, B., Kress, J. S., & Elias, M. J. (2002). *Building learning communities with character.* Alexandria, VA: Association for Supervision and Curriculum Development.

Patti, J., & Tobin, J. (2006). *Smart school leaders: Leading with emotional intelligence* (2nd ed.). Dubuque, IA: Kendall Hunt.

Prinz, R. J., Dumas, J. E., Smith, E. P., & Laughlin, J. E. (2000). The EARLY ALLIANCE prevention trial: A dual design to test reduction of risk for conduct problems, substance abuse, and school failure in childhood. *Controlled Clinical Trials, 21*(3), 286–302.

Sergiovanni, T. J. (2004). Building a community of hope. *Educational Leadership, 61*(8), 33–38.

Tatum, B. D. (2003). *Why are all the black kids sitting together in the cafeteria?* New York: Basic Books.

Ten Eyck, R., Doolan, J., Cram, H., Scannella, A., & Firestone, A. (2006). *An introduction to the New Jersey Professional Development Initiative for School Leaders: A guide to getting started.* Retrieved February 27, 2008, from http://www.nj.gov/education/profdev/pd/leader/guide_files/frame.htm.

Wandersman, A., Keener, D. C., Snell-Johns, J., Miller, R. L., Flaspohler, P., Livet-Dye, M., et al. (2004). Empowerment evaluation: Principles and action. In L. A. Jason, C. B. Keys, Y. Suarez-Balcazar, R. R. Taylor, & M. I. Davis (Eds.), *Participatory community research: Theories and methods in action.* Washington, DC: American Psychological Association.

Zins, J. E., Weissberg, R. P., Wang, M. C., & Walberg, H. J. (Eds.). (2004). *Building academic success on social and emotional learning: What does the research say?* New York: Teachers College Press.

CHAPTER NINE

DEVELOPING AND SUSTAINING LEADERSHIP CAPACITY

NANCY SHIN PASCAL

Audible gasps punctuated the otherwise silent moment immediately following the presentation by a group of Mattoon's teachers at Tuesday's school board meeting. . . . Then the audience broke into applause, needing only that first brave soul to rise and spark a standing ovation.

—*Journal Gazette Times-Courier,*
Mattoon, IL, August 15, 2008

What had these teachers done to invoke such a stunning response? They demonstrated that they had taken ownership of *all* their students' learning by reporting to the school board on the specific challenges and solutions they had addressed last year as a professional learning community (PLC)—thus ensuring that no child truly is left behind. The commitment reflected in their report came as a result of deliberate steps taken by the district leadership in Mattoon, a small district in east-central Illinois. Their intent was to build the leadership capacity necessary to ensure the success of *all* their students and to address the looming retirement of a daunting percentage of the entire staff. Later in this chapter, we will explore how Superintendent Larry Lilly and his administrative team are building sustainable leadership capacity.

The retirement of the Baby Boom generation, though long anticipated, is still creating issues of leadership succession across the United States.

The retirement of the Baby Boom generation, though long anticipated, is still creating issues of leadership succession across the United States. Andy Cole, director of leadership development in Fairfax County, Virginia (the 13th-largest district in the country), has been grappling with this issue for several years. Cole says,

> Seventy percent of our sitting assistant principals and principals retired in a 5-year time period. We had the leadership feeder programs in place to fill these positions, but in the midst of our succession crisis [we] would at times end up "robbing Peter to pay Paul." (Interview with author, April 9, 2008)

Every district has its own formal and informal ways of identifying and engaging aspiring leaders. Enlarging the pool of prospective principals beyond the traditional self-selected candidates is a formidable challenge. The Chicago Public Schools has an entire department devoted solely to principal preparation and development. Medium-sized districts such as Wichita, Kansas, integrate their leadership development efforts with professional development opportunities throughout the district.

An even greater challenge lies in the large numbers of new leaders needed in such a short period of time. The problem is not caused by retirements alone, however; mobility at the principal level is approaching the rate of mobility of superintendents, who average a new position every 3 years or less. As a result, the education community is turning to teachers as the bulwark of school stability in a sea of change. Teachers find themselves leading by default, as new administrators struggle to establish relationships, master information about how the organization operates, keep up with external and district mandates, and manage day-to-day operations.

Education has followed business in applying W. Edwards Deming's revolutionary post–World War II shift to involving workers at the execution level in decision making. Subsequent research has documented that success for schools depends on developing communities of continual learners who are focused on student achievement. Today's leader must let go of the traditional concept of *individual* responsibility for success or failure, and instead embrace sharing leadership to leverage the power of teams to increase student achievement.

Alan Blankstein, author of *Failure Is Not an Option,* sees it like this:

> One way to look at leadership in the building or district is from a team perspective. No one leader will have all the abilities needed to deal with all the complexities of the job. Therefore, one critical component for the leader is to assess others' strengths and build a team accordingly, and to get beyond charismatic leadership, which is not sustainable beyond that leader's tenure. (Interview with author, April 9, 2008)

The concept of teaming has been boosted in education with the popularity of PLCs. Schools try to shift from isolation to collaboration, typically by putting teachers in grade-level or subject-area teams with time to meet together and a mandate to improve student achievement. Taking leadership in these teams is yet another level above participating as a peer—and one that many teachers are reluctant to engage in. In her chapter, "Reconceptualizing the Road Toward Leadership Capacity," Linda Lambert summed it up neatly with a quote from a teacher in her "Women's Ways of Leading" workshop. "But I don't want to be a leader," the teacher said. Asked why not, she replied, "Because they tell others what to do, and they often don't listen." (Linda's treatment of her broader conception of leadership involves reciprocal, purposeful learning in community.)

Given the great demand for leaders, schools and districts need to develop and maintain leadership capacity at all levels simultaneously. We cannot focus on the qualities of a single individual; rather, our task is to identify and foster the defining characteristics of a group that leads. Dennis Sparks calls this concept the "habits of behavior and mind which lead to continuous improvement." It

Given the great demand for leaders, schools and districts need to develop and maintain leadership capacity at all levels simultaneously.

all starts with having a common, defined vision and sharing consistently high moral values.

The themes of vision and values in developing distributed leadership have been woven throughout this volume with international case studies that illustrated each author's perspective. Alma Harris described how successful school leadership can mitigate the effects of poverty with the findings from two studies in England in her chapter, "Against the Odds: Successful Leadership in Challenging Schools." Dean Fink's "Leadership for Mortals: Developing and Sustaining Leaders of Learning" looked at school leadership as a pervasive force with two key features: an absolute commitment to student learning and a set of life-affirming values that sustain leaders through good times and bad.

In "Liberating Leadership Potential: Designing for Leadership Growth," Louise Stoll and David Jackson framed the issue in terms of leadership succession planning. The challenges of change are too great for any one leader, school, district, state, or even nation to tackle alone, they argued, but the challenges can be solved through the employment of networked learning communities.

Maurice Elias reflected on the personal histories of four current practitioner-leaders in "Building Leadership Capacity for School-Based Social-Emotional Learning (SEL): The Trajectory of Young Leaders." The importance of continuous learning, effective communication, facilitative versus authoritarian leadership, optimism, and a prosocial value system described by these young leaders resound throughout this volume.

Fostering and developing leaders who are simultaneously confident and humble in the face of complexity and developing collaborative cultures are the two components of Michael Fullan's sixth "secret of change," described in his chapter, "The Moral Imperative Revisited: Achieving Large-Scale Reform." He reiterates his contention that the moral imperative needs to replace the concept of vision; as he put it, "The six secrets of change embedded with a clear moral purpose can be unstoppable."

A Case Study of Building and Sustaining Leadership

Now we will see how Larry Lilly and his team in Mattoon are meeting the challenge posed by the retirement of 48 leaders with 30-plus years of experience (14 percent of the entire staff) in the next 2 years.

We'll look at the structures and processes used by Mattoon for recruiting future leaders and building leadership capacity at all levels in the district. The efforts of this district and the results they have achieved to date should prove helpful to those seeking to address their own questions of leadership capacity.

The Mattoon area has lost a good many manufacturing jobs but still has a strong rural and agricultural support system. The district serves 3,400 students with 275 certified staff and 175 support staff. Most staff members are concentrated in the ranges of 5 to 10 years and 20 to 25 years of experience; a smaller group is clustered in the 15-year range. A small number of staff members are at the very low and very high levels. Twenty-four percent of the students have individualized education programs (IEPs), double the national average. Free and reduced-price lunch percentages are increasing, with one of four elementary schools over 50 percent; two elementary schools qualify for schoolwide Title I funds. Several years ago, diversity was virtually nonexistent in the district; now it is great enough to move the Mattoon schools into subgroup scrutiny under No Child Left Behind. The number of English language learners (ELL) and of students from homeless families is small but growing.

The administrative team members are going into their fifth year together, led by the superintendent (20 years in the district). Team members include Suzie Smith, director of curriculum and instruction (33 years in the district, and the only self-proclaimed "townie" on the team); Dave Skocy, assistant superintendent for human resources (5 years in Mattoon); and Tom Sherman, business manager (6 years in Mattoon).

When asked to define what leadership is, the team answers with one voice and one word: "relationships." Larry leads by expressing his belief that keen listening to teachers and students and "broadening the tent" under which decisions are made pays big dividends for Mattoon students.

Keen listening to teachers and students and "broadening the tent" under which decisions are made pays big dividends for Mattoon students.

Larry and Suzie were both building administrators when the district turned its junior high into a middle school. Larry remembers it as a time when he was able to let his teachers take on much of the leadership in the change effort:

> They knew a lot more about the culture than I did, and were able to bring people together to solve problems and identify pitfalls

that could cause the reform to go off course. I began to realize that the principal or superintendent sitting in the office and making decisions and setting the vision wasn't about leadership. Leadership began to mean getting folks together to talk about our issues, how we might improve, and where we want to go.

Dave Skocy points to the importance of Larry's ability to provide the space for this change to evolve: "He created a situation where we all became very comfortable sharing the load. 'This is your job description' and 'your responsibility' gave way to blurred lines between roles, and a very fluid environment for doing the work." Interdependence and mutual accountability to the other team members—rather than each to the superintendent and the superintendent to the board—became the norm. With that undergirding of agreement, commitment to a common vision and a common definition of excellence grew throughout the district. Larry retains ultimate responsibility because of his title, and everyone knows that. However, every question about who does what ends with the same answer: 'We work as a team.'"

Bill Harshbarger, a teacher in the district for 35 years, is now a consultant with the district. Bill looks at leadership from the teacher level:

There was a time when if a new administrator came in, everything prior went out the window. Now there is a depth and breadth of knowledge of what exists in the system. Leadership capacity means that we have identified the critical elements in our system and a lot of people who are committed to them, ensuring that the critical elements for success will endure even as leaders change.

Recognizing that nearly one in five of their teachers and administrators were planning to move into retirement in the next 2 years, the Mattoon Central Office Leadership Team created PROJECT 48: Embracing our Legacy to Shape the Future, a comprehensive strategic plan with three goals: (1) fill vacancies; (2) support teachers transitioning into retirement; and (3) maintain and enhance a progressive, student-centered school culture. The leadership team documented past trends and projections for the future regarding student enrollment and teacher employment. They mapped out a recruitment plan and time line to begin in September 2007, with individuals or teams designated to carry out defined activities. They profiled the "Projected Teacher Candidate Pool" (identified in the literature as the "millennial generation") and defined the characteristics of school culture that needed to be considered when screening, interviewing, and employing these candidates. A sample of the plan detail is shown in Table 9.1. (See www.hopefoundation.org for the entire plan.)

How does Mattoon leverage its community relationships to increase the potential leadership pool? Some examples follow.

- *University–school partnership.* Eastern Illinois University has more than 40 student teachers, block students, and practicum students in the district's school buildings each day, giving Mattoon the opportunity to observe potential candidates over time in the classroom.
- *Sharing information with local news media.* Mattoon brought a powerful educational speaker to an all-district professional development day and invited leaders from throughout Coles County to attend the event. The event became "a news event, a big deal," putting the schools front and center in the important things happening in the larger community.
- *Getting involved in community organizations.* Mattoon staff members volunteer in Kiwanis, the YMCA, and coaching summer sports leagues. Central office staff members sit on "boards, boards, all kinds of boards, and more boards."
- *Supporting the development of Leadership Coles County*—a community leadership development program sponsored by the two area Chambers of Commerce.
- *Sharing facilities with other organizations.* School space is used for everything from walking space to basketball camps to training for the electricians' union and the bomb squad to ordaining a priest.
- *Building good working relationships with teachers and support staff associations.* Most recent contract negotiations were concluded in 3 and 4 days, largely because everyone has worked together to create a common vision for excellence. "It may seem counterintuitive in times of tight budgets, but we were

Table 9.1 PROJECT 48: Embracing Our Legacy to Shape the Future (Sample)

September/October 2007	Responsibility
1. Identify known/anticipated hiring needs for 2008–2009 and 2009–2010 school years.	Asst. Supt. of Human Resources
2. Reaffirm District's recruitment goals and hiring guidelines.	Asst. Supt. of Human Resources
3. Reaffirm District's teacher, coach, sponsor job descriptions.	Asst. Supt. of Human Resources
4. Inventory and order recruitment materials.	HR Secretary/Asst. Supt. of Human Resources
5. Analyze future staffing and program needs based on course student enrollment trends, course enrollments, and demographic data.	Asst. Supt. of Human Resources/Asst. Supt. of Business/Superintendent
6. Post known/anticipated vacancies internally. (May post successive years, if needed.)	Asst. Supt. of Human Resources
7. Conduct internal interviews and make recommendations to Asst. Supt. of Human Resources. If needed, post additional internal bids and continue to conduct internal interviews followed by recommendations to the Asst. Supt. of Human Resources.	Recruitment Team
October/November 2007	**Responsibility**
1. Finalize staffing needs based on course enrollment data.	Asst. Supt. of Human Resources/Asst. Supt. of Business/Superintendent
2. Conduct internal interviews and make recommendations to Asst. Supt. of Human Resources. If needed, post additional internal bids and continue to conduct internal interviews followed by recommendations to Asst. Supt. of Human Resources.	Recruitment Team
3. Post known/anticipated vacancies on the District website, other websites (e.g., IASA, ISCPA), and through other media as needed. (May post in successive years, if needed.)	Asst. Supt. of Human Resources

October/November 2007	Responsibility
4. Contact college placement offices with anticipated vacancies.	Recruitment Team
5. Convene Recruitment Team.	Recruitment Team
6. Review and update Recruitment Manual. ○ Review previous school year's initiatives. ○ Determine career/job fairs to attend. ○ Assign team members (and others) to attend. ○ Attend career/job fairs.	Asst. Supt. of Human Resources

able to convince the board that by getting and keeping the best teachers, we actually save money," Tom Sherman reports.

- *Constantly communicating as a central administrative team.* Every morning the other four members of the central administrative team enter the superintendent's office for coffee. They eat lunch together 95 percent of the time. Lines between formal titles or positions are blurred by the fluidity of responsibilities. The team describes their approach to accountability and responsibility as global. All feel responsible for accomplishing the goals of the district and work together to do it.

The central administrative team describes their approach to accountability and responsibility as global. All feel responsible for accomplishing the goals of the district and work together to do it.

- *Actively communicating with the school board.* The Mattoon school board supports what is good for kids, and is in synch with the district's vision that schools are about learning and preparing kids for the future, rather than just test scores.
- *Maintaining positive relationships with current and past employees.* The district knows that word of mouth is the most important factor in recruiting top faculty and staff. Retired teachers and staff, the current workforce of 500, and former staff who have moved to the university level act as emissaries for the schools.

- *Participating in fundraising for local charities.* This fall, for instance, the Mattoon schools had the largest group at the Relay for Life benefit for the American Cancer Society.
- *Providing intergovernmental support.* The district stores the gasoline that fuels local police vehicles for the entire municipality.
- *Recruiting community advisory committees,* most recently to reinstate their agriculture program.

All of these relationships contribute to extremely positive, ongoing public relations for the district, as well as an active communications network. People in the community feel good about their experiences and their relationships with the schools, and they express those feelings to their friends and colleagues. The end result is positive networking at multiple levels. Interested applicants inquire of their friends and colleagues who are familiar with Mattoon and get positive feedback. Friends and colleagues recommend Mattoon to potential candidates whom they feel will be positive additions to the staff. When candidates apply, the Mattoon staff can get honest feedback from their friends and colleagues about potential candidates, and they have developed trusted sources for quality referrals.

From the perspective of human resources, Dave Skocy expresses his approach to recruitment:

> You can go out there and market—put your ads in all the right places, attend job fairs, try to put a nice spin on what you are doing. That is how most school districts go about recruiting. To me, it goes back to the old adage that actions speak louder than words. The focus we have on kids learning and growing is what I truly think has sold this district.

The interdependence of all aspects of leadership development is glaringly evident in a small district like Mattoon. Recruiting, retention, professional development, community involvement, supporting the transition to retirement, and refocusing retired talent all contribute to building leadership capacity in the schools.

Selection Process for Hiring New Teachers

The selection process for hiring teachers has been honed over 15 years based on Vic Cottrell's "Ventures for Excellence" approach (see www.venturesforexcellence.com). During the last 4 years, the district has developed a similar approach for administrators. The process looks for competence in three areas: (1) purpose, (2) human relationship skills, and (3) understanding teaching and learning. An online screener, located on the district's website (www.mattoon .k12.il.us), computes one score; when this score is combined with a seven-question screener on the application form, district staff have two sets of data to help determine which candidates will proceed to the interview process. Dave explains further:

> We trained for the process by watching interviews and having a lot of discussion. The process has a formal protocol, including scoring. The process stresses inter-rater reliability, so as to minimize any one person's potential biases.

During the interview process, "we home in on their purpose and its relation to teaching and learning," Suzie added with conviction. "It's not enough that they just love kids. They also need to understand that their job is to ensure student learning. We find out what they know about what motivates kids, how to make learning applicable and relevant to their lives." Larry continues, "We asked ourselves how to nurture those characteristics in a 23- or 24-year-old teacher as she is hit with the reality of what teaching is."

Identifying Potential Leaders

Once new teachers are in their buildings, the Mattoon approach is to look for people who "don't see limits," according to Suzie. Dave makes the point that

> leadership can emerge at any point in a person's career. It may show itself right away, after families are started, mid-career, or even close to retirement. Some leadership emerges naturally with informal mentoring relationships. It is easy to observe who is respected and who is listened to by peers, and draw on them for leadership.

The intent of the Mattoon approach is to provide as many opportunities as possible to "grow their own" leaders. Examples of such opportunities include

- Tuition waivers for anyone who wants to pursue an education at Eastern Illinois University;
- Tuition reimbursement for master's degree work;
- Sending teachers to professional development trainings;
- Bringing in expert presenters;
- Providing opportunities to serve on internal committees;
- Sponsoring two to four people per year to participate in Coles County Leadership, the joint project mentioned above, sponsored by two adjoining Chambers of Commerce (see www.mattoonchamber.com).

Moreover, the district provides multiple supports for new teachers. In 2004, Mattoon received official approval and recognition by the state of Illinois for its mentoring program. Retired teachers are trained as mentors and peer coaches, who then provide individualized consultation according to the needs of each new teacher. Other facets of the Mattoon program include

- A 3-day orientation prior to the beginning of school;
- Three seminars focusing on the ABCs of teaching during the first year;
- A building-level mentor in addition to the peer coach;
- Follow-up support with the peer coach during the second year of teaching.

The district sponsored a Failure Is Not an Option (FNO): Courageous Leadership for School Success Summit with the HOPE Foundation in August 2007—which was attended by all district employees including secretaries, paraprofessionals, bus drivers, and cafeteria workers—to drive home the message that everyone shares responsibility for the success of every child. They wanted the message to be clear that it would no longer be acceptable to point fingers, and that conversations would now be around how to make the K–12 system work from top to bottom. What had formerly been framed as a "high school graduation" issue was reframed as a whole-system issue that needed input and discussion at every level. Graduation did not depend only on what happened in high school, but was connected to what happens from the day a preschooler enters the system and works his or her way through each grade level. All district employees committed to using the six principles of FNO as a system for organizing district and building initiatives vertically and horizontally. Finally, everyone in the Mattoon schools heard the message that the expertise needed was already within the district, if the proper forums for sharing and implementation were created.

———————— ❧ ————————

Everyone in the Mattoon schools heard the message that the expertise needed was already within the district, if the proper forums for sharing and implementation were created.

Focus Groups for Teachers Sponsored by Local Foundation

Another effort at the high school level (instigated 4 years ago in partnership with the Lumpkin Family Foundation) was the creation of focus groups of teachers. All teachers were invited to participate in the focus groups. A large portion of the faculty met routinely to talk about a variety of issues, including schedules, discipline, curriculum and instruction, student services, and daily instructional problems. They created a PLC group—which got right to the heart of instruction in the classroom—that met every month to talk specifically about the transition to building a professional learning community.

"The foundation gave us money as well as advice and support," Bill Harshbarger said. "We could actually pay our teachers to go to meetings where they were going to learn things they needed to learn."

However, Mary Eddy, a consultant with the Lumpkin Foundation, expressed her frustration with efforts to build leadership capacity at the high school through these focus groups. Eddy said, "They did do wonderful things, including engaging faculty, but with the important exception of increasing the graduation rate, the broad summary is that performance is flat over the 4 years we've been working."

Eddy also worked with the administrative team to build support for a radically different method of developing leaders by learning together in teams: the HOPE Foundation's Courageous Leadership Academy (CLA). In her opinion, the potential of this academy to impact student achievement is promising.

The Courageous Leadership Academy is intended to build consistency within and between schools by creating a professional learning community among leadership teams, allowing them to examine and improve instructional practices in a truly collaborative culture. The CLA uses best-practice professional development standards, as defined by the National Staff Development Council.

The CLA embeds new learning into daily practice. Group sessions model activities for teams to practice and then implement in their own buildings.

Modeling Learning From the Top Down

An important piece of building leadership capacity is modeling learning at the top. The Mattoon administrative team exhibited this with their consultants. Dave Skocy reflected this attitude:

> Having consultants like Mary and Bill in the district to work with the district leadership has been a catalyst for this team to grow professionally, by posing questions that challenge our thinking and keeping us focused on teaching and learning, engaging leaders in questions that force us to think out of the box.

It takes courage to say, "We're not getting the results we want. Our students deserve more and we can do better." Mattoon leaders have shown the moral vision that impels change. According to Mary, "Their honesty and readiness to engage in the interest of students is continually inspiring. Mattoon educators express the humility of themselves being learners."

Suzie Smith sums up Mattoon's vision and values this way:

> It's been a wonderful experience to see so many people in our district learn this year. You will never ever say that anything that we are doing is to raise test scores. We've been fortunate that any change that we have ever made was never for something as insulting as a test score; it's about our children, our grandchildren, our community.

Linda Lambert's research found that high leadership-capacity schools are learning communities that amplify leadership for all, learning for all, and success for all. One key factor is the creation of a system that employs "broad participation with skillful leadership on everyone's part. This schema leads to high engagement and commitment by educators to the priorities set for student and adult learning" (Lambert, Chapter 2, this volume).

DEVELOPING TEACHER LEADERSHIP

The concept of learning communities softens the boundaries of hierarchical accountability. In a traditional hierarchy, teachers are evaluated by the principal, who is then responsible for coaching each teacher on how he or she needs to improve. In a learning community, teachers are accountable to their peers, and they work together as a team to learn from each other. The principal becomes a facilitator of learning and coaches the team members on how to help each other teach more effectively, rather than directly coaching each teacher. This shifts the burden of leadership to teachers, who then take ownership of the continuous improvement process—analyzing the effectiveness of current instructional practices, determining a plan for necessary professional development to improve student outcomes, monitoring implementation of new strategies, and repeating the process until all students are successful.

Developing teacher leadership is a very practical response to the harsh realities of instability of leadership at the top, escalating student needs, and decreasing resources. The use of current personnel helps to mitigate these realities. Harnessing the power of untapped leadership potential in teachers makes sense from many perspectives.

Developing teacher leadership is a very practical response to the harsh realities of instability of leadership at the top, escalating student needs, and decreasing resources.

Student learning happens at the classroom level. As we have learned from the business world, those closest to the process know it best, and including those at the execution level increases the effectiveness of the outcome and the buy-in of those charged with implementing the outcome, as well as decreases the resistance of peers. The value of peer expertise and voluntary contributions cannot be overestimated. As teachers become comfortable in their role as decision makers, they begin to take more ownership of their students' learning. They become accustomed to looking outside for best-practice solutions and making data-informed decisions. They learn how to give and to get support from teammates, as the anxiety of change subsides. Spirits are lifted as hard work pays off in improved results. Working on a high-performing team is exhilarating, and energy increases as the environment becomes more positive.

What we've seen in Mattoon is that sustainability of student success increases with breadth and depth of leadership. The absence of one or another member of a team does not slow the team. Representatives can seek new ideas by visiting other teams or other schools or by engaging in professional development. Transitions are easier to navigate, since the entire team shares the load when someone leaves.

As the culture begins to change, practices grow roots that are strong and difficult to uproot. New faculty are smoothly integrated into the culture, as they have a whole team supporting them. Principals become facilitators of change, guiding and coaching rather than having all the responsibility for making things happen. They can concentrate on managing the many moving parts in the life of the school, as teachers take ownership of instruction.

In short, relationships become more professional. Conversations focus on professional practice and how to improve it. Building professional learning communities benefits the students, the faculty, the administration, and the community at large.

In the words of one of the teachers who presented that night of August 15 at the Mattoon school board meeting, "If we are passionate about students' understanding, we can do a better job of educating them. It's really trying to solve the problem of educating all the children who show up." He quoted Antoine de Saint-Exupéry, the French author and aviator: "If you want to build a ship, don't herd people together to collect wood and don't assign them tasks and work, but rather, teach them to long for the endless immensity of the sea."

INDEX

CORWIN
PRESS

The Corwin logo—a raven striding across an open book—represents the union of courage and learning. Corwin is committed to improving education for all learners by publishing books and other professional development resources for those serving the field of PreK–12 education. By providing practical, hands-on materials, Corwin continues to carry out the promise of its motto: **"Helping Educators Do Their Work Better."**

The HOPE Foundation logo stands for Harnessing Optimism and Potential Through Education. The HOPE Foundation helps to develop and support educational leaders over time at district- and state-wide levels to create school cultures that sustain all students' achievement, especially low-performing students.

American Association of School Administrators

The American Association of School Administrators, founded in 1865, is the professional organization for over 13,000 educational leaders across America. AASA's mission is to support and develop effective school system leaders who are dedicated to the highest quality public education for all children.